C0-ASB-214

LOOKING
UNTO
JESUS

LOOKING UNTO JESUS

Help for living out Christian values

George B. Wall

Judson Press® **Valley Forge**

LOOKING UNTO JESUS

Copyright © 1986
Judson Press, Valley Forge, PA 19482-0851

All rights reserved. No part of this publication may be reproduced, stored in a retrieval system, or transmitted in any form or by any means, electronic, mechanical, photocopying, recording, or otherwise, without the prior permission of the copyright owner, except for brief quotations included in a review of the book.

Bible quotations in this volume are from the Revised Standard Version of the Bible copyrighted 1946, 1952 © 1971, 1973 by the Division of Christian Education of the National Council of the Churches of Christ in the U.S.A., and used by permission.

Library of Congress Cataloging-in-Publication Data
Wall, George B.
   Looking unto Jesus: help for living out Christian values.

   Bibliography: p.
   1. Christian life—1960-   . 2. Jesus Christ—
Example.   I. Title.
BV4501.2.W3224   1986   248.4   85-23188
ISBN 0-8170-1098-X

The name JUDSON PRESS is registered as a trademark in the U.S. Patent Office.
Printed in the U.S.A.

The quotation on page 40 is from Epictetus, *The Enchiridion,* in W. T. Jones, *Approaches to Ethics* (New York: McGraw-Hill Book Company, Inc., © 1962), p. 82a, and is reproduced with permission.

Contents

1 • Reflections on God's Kingdom and This Age
7

2 • Jesus and Social Convention
23

3 • Jesus and the Affective Life (Part One)
37

4 • Jesus and the Affective Life (Part Two)
63

5 • Jesus and Individual Attention
79

6 • Jesus and Plain Speaking
107

7 • The Kingdom, Culture, and Persons
119

Discussion Questions
129

Notes
141

1

Reflections on God's Kingdom and This Age

In the latter part of the nineteenth century, "Hillary" and "Henry" were sent by a geographical society to explore and map remote regions of southeastern Alaska. They traveled by canoe up the Chilkat River to the Tlingit village of Klukwan. The weather had been uncomfortable, with intermittent snow flurries and a biting wind. Now they were within sight of the village, and the anticipation of rest, refreshment, and warmth stimulated them to paddle with increased vigor. As they brought their canoe to shore, they noticed some unusual activity in the village. An event of significance seemed to be taking place.

Hillary and Henry approached the village, noticing that a crowd was gathering about one of the houses. With some hesitation and anxiety they made their way to the house, but they drew little attention. The villagers were completely absorbed by what was going on at the house. Suddenly a villager sallied forth from the house in full native regalia and launched into a lengthy speech. Since Hillary and Henry had only a rudimentary command of the language, they did not understand most of what was said. (Later they learned that the man was recounting his history, telling of his mighty deeds as well as those of his ancestors.) After finishing his tale, the speaker grabbed his spear, began to sing a song, and then feigned an attack on one of the men in the crowd. The man who was being attacked quickly raised his spear and thrust it into his attacker, killing him!

Hillary and Henry did not know what to make of this whole affair, although they rightly surmised that a ritual execution had taken place. In order to get the complete story, they approached a villager standing by them who spoke a little English. What crime had the man committed? The man had not committed any crime. What? They could not believe their ears. If the man had not committed a crime, why was he killed? The Tlingits certainly would not go around killing innocent people arbitrarily.[1]

No, the Tlingits did not go around killing innocent people arbitrarily, but they had no hesitation about killing an innocent person under special circumstances. The Tlingit social structure was grounded in clan solidarity and individual status within the clan. Crimes against a clan member were not considered individual losses but clan losses. Moreover, the clan of the victim required the sacrifice of an individual of the same status from the clan of the criminal. If a person of low rank in one clan killed a person of high rank in another, a high-ranking member of the criminal's clan must suffer death instead of the criminal. This is what had happened in the case Hillary and Henry had witnessed.

Hillary and Henry quickly discovered that the Tlingit system of punishment worked well to deter crime. Yet the system jarred their moral sensibilities. Punishing the innocent, in their opinion, was a fundamental injustice to be avoided even at considerable social cost.

Yet the Tlingits were not influenced by these moral sensibilities. What were Hillary and Henry getting excited about? The Tlingits were following the way of their world— and that was that!

The Two Cultures

The Tlingits freely practiced a custom that many Westerners would find highly questionable, if not immoral. Yet the Tlingits considered the practice of the custom perfectly natural. If pressed for an explanation of the practice, the average Tlingit would have truly replied: "It's the way of our world." In other words, the practice was simply one of their customs—and customs are to be followed, not questioned.

Few societies are arranged so as to provide a constant review and evaluation of either their customs or the values underlying the customs. In fact, customs seen as unnatural, odd, or bizarre by one group will invariably be seen as thoroughly natural by the group following the customs. The Christian thinker Blaise Pascal says:

> What are our natural principles but principles of custom? In children they are those which they have received from the habits of their fathers. . . . A different custom will cause different natural principles. This is seen in experience; and if there are some natural principles ineradicable by custom, there are also some customs opposed to nature, ineradicable by nature. . . .[2]

Pascal also says, "The nature of man is wholly natural. . . . There is nothing he may not make natural; there is nothing natural he may not lose."[3] A practice that is continually articulated and reinforced from childhood by the family, as well as by the educational and religious institutions of a society, will not be viewed as anything but natural, whether the practice be scarring the body or face or piling on top of one another to assure capture of a piece of inflated pigskin.

Customs are like the roots of a tree, spreading into the subsoil, twisting about rocks and other roots. Tearing out a custom would mean tearing at major institutions and corollary practices. In Tlingit society, for example, the punishment of the innocent was intertwined with the clan and status system of the society. Changing the practice would have meant changing these major aspects of the society.

Our customs seem natural and right to us; they are root-ed in the major institutions of our society. These facts are essential for us to grasp if we are to comprehend the call of Jesus to the new life of the kingdom. We are confronted with two radically different cultures—the culture of our society and the culture of the kingdom. The culture of our society is as natural to us as breathing, for we have been conditioned by it from birth. As a result, we see our cul-ture—the basic values, beliefs, and practices of our soci-ety—as healthy and good. We in the United States hear often that ours is a Christian country—a bromide dis-pensed, astonishingly, by clergy as well as politicians. Fur-ther, our alleged adversary the Soviet Union is pictured as evil, the "focus of evil." Obviously, if the Soviet Union is the focus of evil, we in the West, and in the United States especially, must be the focus of good, an idea which, from the biblical standpoint, borders on the preposterous. According to the New Testament the age in which we live is an evil age (Galatians 1:4). By no rule of reasonable biblical interpretation can the evil of our age be limited to certain nations. All nations participate in the pollution of the age. Our culture, as well as all others, is not well-rooted in the reign of Christ. On the contrary, our culture is worldly, a culture rooted in self-centeredness (2 Cor-inthians 5:15) and characterized by the "lust of the flesh, the lust of the eyes, and the pride of life" (1 John 2:15–17).

The idea that our culture is basically evil is probably a bit jarring to us, if not downright shocking—and not un-expectedly, for we have been acculturated. That is, we have acquired the values, practices, and beliefs that dis-tinguish our society. We have absorbed our culture from infancy and therefore consider it natural and appropriate. Generally, we do not even think about our culture—the customs we follow, the values we espouse, the beliefs we hold; rather, we function from habit. As slaves of habit, we find it difficult to accept the accusation that our cultural system is to be characterized as evil. Yet Paul is unambiguous in his statement that this age is evil (Galatians 1:4) and that because it is, we are not to conform to it. (In Romans 12:1,2 the term translated "world" is the same as the term translated "age" in Galatians 1:4.) Moreover, Paul was not referring mainly to the evil of the Roman form of government. Actually, the Roman form of government, considered strictly as a political system, was capable of providing excellent rule (embodied by the reign of Augustus, as well as the reigns of the "Good Emperors" Nerva, Trajan, Hadrian, Antoninus Pius, Marcus Aurelius). Nothing in Paul's statement indicates that his focus was the Roman political system.

Admittedly, evil is expressed through political systems. The Soviet Union, however, hardly has a corner on the "lust of the flesh, the lust of the eyes, and the pride of life." Indeed, the Western democracies are senior competitors in the pursuit of these evils. In short, "worldliness" is expressed in all societies, regardless of political systems. *Our culture, taken as a whole, is dominated by values that conflict with the values of God's kingdom.* The sooner we who profess Christ grasp this fact, the sooner we will grasp the extent of God's judgment on our society, the extent to which we need God's grace, and the extent of the demands of the reign of Christ.

In spite of what has just been said, it is true that some values in our society and in others have been tempered by the values of the kingdom. The people of God are a remnant in every society. (The assumption here is that statistics concerning church membership are by no means an accurate measure of the children of the kingdom.) However, they simply lack the political and judicial clout to instill systematically the values of the kingdom in the laws and institutions of their societies. In democratic countries the children of God have often been able to condition some of the values of their country with the values of the kingdom, but the conditioning has not been extensive enough to bring the laws and institutions consistently into line with the values of the kingdom. In addition, because of their minority status, Christians do not constitute a pervasive enough presence and pressure to move areas outside the law systematically in the direction of kingdom values. (For example, sexual attitudes in the United States, as well as attitudes toward violence, represent serious drifts from the attitudes expressed by Christ.)

The truth remains, then, that every society, including ours, falls short of submitting itself systematically to the reign of Christ; or more accurately, the failure to submit to the reign of Christ is so extensive in every society that the dominant value system is in conflict with the value system of the kingdom of God. Every society presents us with a gap, a chasm, between its culture and the culture of the kingdom. Two cultures in conflict persist in evey society.

The Culture of the Kingdom

So far we have referred only to the values of the kingdom. The time has come to define them. The fundamental values of the kingdom were summed up by Jesus in two rules: Love God with your whole being and love your neighbor as yourself (Mark 12:18-31).

The Value of Persons

In order to understand the significance of loving relationships, we need to take a brief journey to the springs of philosophy and theology that water the roots of our faith. The first observation on this journey is that biblical theism is a form of personal theism—that is, God is conceived of as a personal Spirit. The emphasis of this observation is on the word "personal."

Probably the easiest way to approach an understanding of that word is to begin where we have our best grasp of what a person is, namely, with ourselves. We are clearly persons, whereas our pets—our dogs, our cats, our canaries, our parakeets, our monkeys, our snakes—are not. Why not? What do they lack that we have?

To begin with, they lack our ability to communicate. Animal behaviorists have spent many years teaching monkeys to communicate on a very elementary level. However, we may say without fear of contradiction that no investigator has discussed with the monkeys, or is ever likely to discuss with them, the merits of democracy over totalitarianism, the feelings one has when viewing the Sistine Chapel, Nat King Cole's rendition of "Mona Lisa," the basketball dynasty of the Boston Celtics, or the design argument for God. In short, the gap between animal and human communication is in reality a gigantic chasm. The ability to communicate is rooted in rational capacity, and monkeys, along with other animals, do not compare with humans in this respect.

Another aspect of our identity as human beings is that of morality. We make decisions on the grounds of right and wrong, feel guilt, and are moved by praise and blame. Our ability to function morally, like our ability to communicate, is rooted in our highly developed rational capacity.

A further feature by which we distinguish ourselves as persons is our capacity for self-consciousness. Again, experiments with monkeys have shown an elementary awareness of self. (Monkeys can recognize themselves in a mirror.) Yet recognizing oneself in a mirror is a galaxy away from the human capacity of self-consciousness, expressing itself in such diverse ways as Descartes's "I think, therefore I am," the experiences of guilt and loneliness, concern over self-image, reflections on the past ("I never had as much fun as I did yesterday"), and so on. Thus, we may say that a personal being is also a being who is self-conscious on a fairly advanced level.

If a person is distinguished by the traits mentioned above, then God is certainly personal. The God of the Bible communicates as Creator with creatures, revealing aspects of the Creator's being, will, and purpose. The God of the Bible is also a moral being, having among other qualities, those of justice, righteousness, truth, and love. Indeed, God is viewed by many as the very foundation of morality. Finally, the God of the Bible is clearly a self-conscious being. For example, "I am the LORD your God, who brought you out of the land of Egypt" (Exodus 20:2); and, "I am the LORD, that is my name; my glory I give to no other" (Isaiah 42:8).

Since the God of the Bible is the fundamental reality of the universe and, in addition, is personal, we can conclude that personhood is a fundamental value in the universe. Certainly God values the personal. The crown of God's creation was a person, a being made in God's own image. It is of little wonder that God chose to come to earth in the form of a human person—Jesus Christ.

The Value of Loving Relationships

In addition to the rational capacities that they have, human beings are surely made for relationship. Indeed, we see God immediately relating to humankind lovingly (conversing with the man about his well-being) and devising a scheme (marriage) whereby males and females can relate lovingly to one another (see Genesis 2). The unambiguous message is that persons and loving relationships are the fundamental values of the universe. In fact, if God has created other personal beings besides men, women, and angels, God must value for them exactly what is valued for us, for God cannot change.

Not all religions espouse similar values. Eastern religions generally take an impersonal approach to God. For example, the Hindu God Brahman is referred to as "the unspeaking, the unconcerned" and is often portrayed as a great river, sweeping everything along in its current. Moreover, the highest values in Hinduism are not those of persons or loving relationships; instead, the highest value is release from or rising above oneself into union with the divine. This union is a merger with the divine, not a communion between selves.

Embedded in the tapestry of personal theism is the philosophical backdrop for the kingdom value of loving relationships. If we believe in a personal God, we are not strangers in a universe inhospitable to loving relationships. Just the opposite is true. The universe, at the level of the divine, is supportive of loving relationships. This thought can help us to survive the daily buffeting by our "worldly" culture (Colossians 3:1–2), a culture suffused with the impersonal, the uncaring, the unloving.

Yet the extent to which our culture departs from the culture of loving relationships may escape us, for, as we have observed, we have been acculturated. From our earliest years we have been taught to march to the value-beat of our culture; we have been taught that doing so will bring us "the good life." However, many of the values to which we march—power, profit, pleasure, wealth, status, comfort, physical strength, physical attractiveness, fame, success—may be anything but conducive to the truly good life as measured by the kingdom value of loving relationships.

Perhaps focusing on our criteria of success will help us to see more clearly the alien nature (from a kingdom standpoint) of our cultural values. In sports, or to be more specific, in track and field, who are the successful people? Carl Lewis, Edwin Moses, Joan Benoit, Mary Decker Slaney, Valery Briscoe Hooks, Roger Kingdom—these are people who immediately come to mind. Why? Because they win and because they earn the most money. In 1984 Carl Lewis brought in $783,000; Edwin Moses, $617,000; Joan Benoit, $402,000; and Mary Decker Slaney, $355,000. We measure success in sports by winning and by money. Yet what about my friend Sterling? He has lowered his time in five kilometer racing by two minutes and is now running at his peak. His best finish was in a downpour with driving wind; he came in third out of a field of five.

But is he successful? Not by our cultural standards. Even though Sterling has improved and is fulfilling his potential, he is not successful because he does not win.

By kingdom standards, however, Sterling is a resounding success. The parable of the talents teaches clearly that those who grow and reach their potential are successful. Moreover, growth and striving to reach limits, in the broadest sense, is crucial to relationships. Growth expands the capacity to share and provides interest, adventure, and excitement in a relationship.

Unfortunately, our cultural criteria of success obscure both the value of fulfilling one's potential as a person and the value of seeking loving relationships. Jim Ryun states that he was "embittered for quite a little while" after his accident in the 1,500-meter trials at the 1972 Olympics. His hopes for a gold medal were dashed as he and another runner crashed to the track. Failing to get "the gold," the ultimate measure of success, often devastates one's life. Ryun knew of another value system, for he had a Christian commitment. Yet the cultural value of winning was so deeply imbedded that for a while he could think of nothing but his loss. Fortunately, Ryun was able to work through his bitterness and achieve self-acceptance and peace.[4]

Success, as measured by our culture, is only one of a vast array of values in our society running counter to the values of the kingdom. Our task as Christians is a formidable one. As Jesus said, "the gate is narrow and the way is hard, that leads to life" (Matthew 7:14). Or as Paul said, we are in a war, a war with all the hosts of wickedness (Ephesians 6:10-17). These hosts employ, among other things, cultural values that are antithetical to and destructive of the kingdom value of loving relationships.

Starting Point: Relationship with God

Having noted the gap between kingdom and many cultural values and having considered the fact that our cultural values are normally as natural to us as breathing, we need to look more closely at the kingdom value of loving relationships. We have observed that the value is a twofold value, including relationship with God and relationship with others. The focus of our study will be relationship with others. Specifically, we shall look at Jesus in order to grasp more firmly and concretely exactly what relating lovingly to others means. First, though, we will consider the connection between relationship with God and relationship with others.

The Bible places a clear priority on humankind's relationship with God. The major tragedy of the fall is alienation from God. Instead of joyfully walking with God in the garden, God's creatures cower in hiding, desperately and futilely trying to cover the nakedness of their alienation with leaves. The significance of the cross is that God in Christ has provided for reconciliation; the leaves can go! Indeed, the essential meaning of eternal life is reconciliation and fellowship, not endless existence. Jesus said, "This is eternal life, that they *know* [italics added] thee the only true God, and Jesus Christ whom thou hast sent" (John 17:3). Eternal life is simply knowing God in the relational sense (the sense common throughout Scripture), of having fellowship or communion with, of being close to. Eternal life is like drinking fresh water from a flowing spring as opposed to stale water from a holding tank (Jeremiah 2:13); it is life lived in fellowship with the Divine, the Creator of heaven and earth, the God and Father of the Lord Jesus Christ.

We should not suppose that knowing God is something that happens all at once, say, at conversion. We do not come to know any person fully in an instant and most definitely not the infinite God. Part of the excitement of the Christian life is the adventure of seeking an ever-expanding awareness of God and of God's presence. One widespread affliction of modern men and women is *ennui*, or boredom, which is rooted in a repetitive materialistic lifestyle. A more devastating critique of a lifestyle can hardly be imagined. Listen, for example, to the words of Daisy in F. Scott Fitzgerald's *The Great Gatsby*: "You see, I think everything's terrible anyhow. . . . Everybody thinks so—the most advanced people. And I *know*. I've been everywhere and seen everything and done everything. . . . Sophisticated—God, I'm sophisticated!"[5] Been everywhere and seen everything and done everything. Again we hear Daisy say, "What'll we do with ourselves this afternoon . . . and the day after that, and the next thirty years?"[6]

What'll we do? Surely, we, the children of the kingdom, can plumb the depths of the infinite God. There is no boredom in the pursuit of the Divine.

Relationship with God, however, is not without responsibilities. The person who has experienced the new quality of life found in relationship with God cannot but wish to extend this pursuit of relationship to others. Experience with God has lifted the fog of self-centeredness, revealing the beauty and splendor of loving relationships. Having seen, the true believer cannot, whatever the temporary reversions into opaqueness, be satisfied with anything else. He or she has discovered an internal void—a void for the Other and for others. Thus, John writes, "Beloved, let us love one another; for love is of God, and he who loves is born of God and *knows* [italics added] God" (1 John 4:7). Coming into relationship with God is nothing short of a rebirth, a rebirth from the deadness of self-centered living (2 Corinthians 5:15) to the new life (2 Corinthians 5:17) of loving relationships. On the other hand, persons who continue in the deadness of self-centeredness, whose lives are not quests for loving relationships, have just not met God, whatever their religious activities and associations. "He who does not love does not know God; for God is love" (1 John 4:8).

Thus, contact with the Divine is not an experience insulated from the rest of life. Relationship with God brings love and newness to life. One reason why this relationship makes all things new (2 Corinthians 5:17), changing life from focus on self to focus on loving relationships, is that relationship with God inevitably changes our view of ourselves. A major consequence of alienation from God is a degraded sense of self-worth. Indeed, a weak or absent sense of self-worth is at the heart of poor relationships. Jesus said, "Love your neighbor as yourself." The person who does not love himself or herself will simply not be able to love others. In fact, that person will probably engage in some form of the "put-down game," a game especially evident among teenagers.

Janie came to me practically in tears. She was a pretty girl with a vivacious personality; yet she was not able to break into the "in" groups in her junior high school. She could not get into the prestige clubs, nor could she attain a position as a cheerleader. Worst of all, though, Janie was excluded in "little ways" by the "big people" on campus. When she approached a group of them, they would cut off their whispering of the latest gossip or off-color stories, remarking that she just wouldn't get what they were talking about; she just wasn't sophisticated enough, not grown-up enough. Janie was crushed.

Fortunately, Janie had enough reserves to appreciate what I said to her: "Janie, do you know that you're really important to me, to a whole lot of other people and, yes, to God? You're very attractive, you have real abilities, and you're lots of fun. You know what's wrong with those kids who are putting you down? They really don't like themselves! In order to feel good about themselves, they need someone beneath them. Now isn't that kind of sick? Does the person who really likes himself or herself have to put anybody else down?"

Janie got the message. She firmed up her grip on her self-worth and began to develop into a self-confident young woman who related well to others.

The good news of our faith, the news that God accepts us in Christ, forgiving us unreservedly, is news that must restore a flagging sense of self-worth. We have been accepted by the Creator of heaven and earth, so who cares whether some human tries to put us down? How can we fail to be worth something when we are the image and glory of God (1 Corinthians 11:7)? That is why we can relate to God. Contact with God in Christ is potent medicine for a diseased sense of self-worth.

Although our relationship with God is pivotal to our sense of self-worth and hence to our relationships with others, our relationship with God can be affected for good or ill by what is happening with others. In short, the connection between relationship with God and relationship with others is reciprocal.

Jim came into my office considerably agitated. He was a young Christian but had consistently shown signs of growth. He seemed to be especially sensitive to and appreciative of his acceptance in Christ. No wonder, then, that he was agitated, for he felt distant from God, his prayers seeming "to bounce off the ceiling." A few moments of probing revealed that Jim and his father had butted heads over an important business matter. Jim's father, a non-Christian, was advocating a business deal that was blatantly unethical. Jim, to follow his Lord, was not about to approve the deal. The result was a sharp, angry exchange with his father. This exchange was especially hurtful to Jim because his father had gone on a tirade against Jim's newfound faith, calling him a religious fanatic. The reason for Jim's feelings of distance from God immediately became clear: Jim felt distant from his father (for whom he cared deeply) and had generalized this feeling of distance to God. What Jim needed to see was that God's acceptance of him had not altered even a fraction. The alteration was in Jim's relationship with his father.

In cases such as Jim's, we must be clear about what is going on with God, as opposed to what is going on with others. The complexity of the dynamics of relationships— how one relationship affects or is affected by another— along with our struggle to understand the human psyche, makes clarity about what is going on anything but easy.

However, the object of this study is not to solve the puzzles of the human psyche or unravel the mysteries of human relationships. Having noted the effects of relationship with God on relationship with others and *vice versa*, we are now ready for a careful look at how Jesus related to others in order that we might see a clearer picture of truly loving relationships.

Conclusion

Most of us are acculturated thoroughly. The values of our culture are deposited in the deepest layers of our thinking, attitudes, and behavior. We give little thought to these values, tacitly accepting them, rather than letting the light of critical evaluation shine on them. But if we are to benefit from this study, we must decide to descend to these layers to dig out the deposited values and bring them up into the light. Only then can we see how they relate to the values of the kingdom.

Moreover, what is true for the values of our culture is also true for the beliefs and dogmas of our particular religious tradition. Our beliefs about Jesus and the Christian life have come from a variety of sources—from parents, lay teachers, clergy, current social opinion, popular books, scholarly books, personal study of the Scriptures, hymns, and so on. In short, what we believe is a strange amalgam of unexamined or superficially examined church dogma or current opinion. As a result, we come to Jesus with colored glasses; we see him through the lenses of already-formed beliefs. An honest study of Jesus requires the admission that much of what we believe about Jesus is sheer prejudice—unexamined dogma—and that total removal of the glasses is difficult, if not impossible. We must be radically open to see what the Gospels teach about Jesus and radically willing to shape our beliefs and lives accordingly.

Earlier we spoke of the boredom that haunts modern men and women and of how the quest of God is anything but boring. The same can be said of the quest for loving relationships. It is anything but boring. It is high adventure—risky, perilous, demanding. Yet who would not trade the humdrum for the exciting? The call of Jesus is to risk all for loving relationships.

2

Jesus and Social Convention

Joe had spent his early years getting into minor scrapes with the law, graduating at the age of seventeen to armed robbery, for which he was sent to a special correctional farm for youth. While at the farm he committed himself to Christ. After release he immediately searched for a church in which to become active, finding one of about 250 members on the fringe of the inner city. And active he did become. He was present for every youth Bible study, prayer meeting, and social event. He never missed a church worship service. When an opportunity to testify arose, he was the first on his feet. Although a young Christian, he seemed to be outdistancing the other young people of the church, not to mention many of the adults.

Naturally, everyone was pleased to see this "fine young man" so active and so serious about the faith—until parents began to learn of Joe's background. Then the gossip began. "Did you know that he did time? I hear it was for armed robbery." "Yes, and he was probably also into drugs." "What do you think about his influence on the youth?" "I sure don't want him going out with my daughter." "I hear he's been dating Maggie. . . ."

The adults' attitude toward Joe cooled as did the attitude

of many youth, obviously because of parental pressure.

Joe was puzzled. He had been taught that the church was a forgiving and accepting community. Yet one time he stated that he found more acceptance at the correctional farm than in the church. Unless a radical change took place in the attitude of the church, it was probable that Joe would soon be back in prison. But no change took place. Joe was treated with bare civility. He began to drift back to his old friends and was shortly back in prison.

Joe is simply one of the many people in our society who are placed on the fringe by social convention. All we have to say is "ex con" and we exclude the person from our normal set of contacts.

A forceful illustration of social attitudes is found in the reactions of people to the proposal to put a halfway house in their neighborhood for parolees. An immense hue and cry goes up. The house represents a threat to the fine citizens of the community, some of whom have probably engaged in questionable activities themselves. If the house is for those who pose little or no threat—the mentally handicapped, the alcoholic, the emotionally disturbed—then the shrill cry of reduced property values will sound. The fact is that social convention simply excludes whole groups from "nice society," the society of the "solid tax-paying citizen." This convention is hardly surprising for the children of this age who are seeking an undisturbed, comfortable lifestyle; but when the convention is followed by those who call themselves the children of God, by those who have committed themselves to follow the One who risked all for human redemption, then something has surely gone awry.

Joe made his move to the church, supposing that it was a different sort of community. Some of its members were different and fought long and hard for a change of attitude in the church; yet they did not prevail. This church needed, among other things, a clear vision of the demands of Jesus.

The question, then, is "What did Jesus do about social

convention?" How did he relate to people whom social convention relegated to the fringes? We shall begin the study of these questions by seeing how Jesus related to women.

Women

Women were in an inferior position in early Jewish society, being excluded from status positions and activities. One might argue that the exclusion represented only a division of roles. The woman's role was that of housewife and mother, a role which, if fully performed, simply made performing any other role impossible. The argument is supported by a contemporary Jewish writer, who remarks that "the distinction between the sexes was based on a functional division of tasks, which are seen as separate but equal."[1] However, the same writer also notes that "men persisted in regarding themselves as the more fortunte sex, privileged to fulfill a greater number of precepts; this is attested to by the benediction recited each morning in which a man praises God for not having made him a woman."[2]

A moment's reflection is sufficient to remind us that a mother does not have her children in the household forever; neither is being a housewife a totally demanding task at all times. In any case, women were excluded from much more than could ever by justified by their roles as housewives and mothers. Perhaps we could admit that their roles might exclude them from the priesthood, but why should it push them to the fringes of religious duties and privileges? Why did women not recite the *shema* (the Jewish confession of faith; see Deuteronomy 6:4,5) or wear phylacteries? Further, why did women not have certain religious privileges like men had, privileges such as entering fully into the worship of the temple (women were restricted to the forecourt of the temple) or being counted as part of a quorum in a synagogue? Or why were girls not regularly instructed, as were boys, in the Scriptures and rabbinic teachings? To be sure, a study of the Scriptures required learning the ancient Hebrew language, yet learning domestic skills was hardly so time-consuming that it eliminated the possibility of girls studying language and Scripture. We can read of exceptional cases of women who became learned in the Scriptures and rabbinic teachings. One noteworthy case is that of Beruriah, daughter of a rabbi and wife of a rabbi, both eminent in their time. She

> is said to have studied three hundred talmudic topics in a day, and to have spent three years on the Book of Genealogies. She even gave opinions on points of law, and on one such, a question of clean or unclean, Rabbi [her husband] approved her decision, though it went counter to the prevailing opinion of the learned.[3]

Not one word is ever said to the effect that Beruriah was not an adequate wife or mother.

Not only were women in an inferior position religiously but they were also in an inferior position legally. In Deuteronomy 24:1, for example, we read that a husband could divorce his wife, but not vice versa. (We should not think, however, that divorce for trivial reasons was rampant in the Jewish community. A degree of restraint was imposed on the husband by the sum of money he must give to his wife upon divorcing her, as well as the general rabbinic disapproval of divorce.) One fault for which he could divorce was barrenness. In fact, the husband had the duty to divorce his wife if she bore no children after ten years. God's command was to be fruitful and multiply. The onus of barrenness was always on the wife.

Being inferior in matters of position and law was bad enough for women, but their situation was made even worse by their practical exclusion from the society of men. Women were viewed as a threat to the continence of men. The rabbis were insistent that men must keep their distance from women, as the following passage indicates.

> Under no circumstances should a man walk behind a woman, not even his own wife. One who walks behind a woman crossing a stream has no share in the World to Come. One who pays

money out of his hand into a woman's so as to get a look at her, though he have as much learning and good works as our master Moses, will not get off from condemnation to hell. . . . A man should not gaze on a handsome woman, even an un-married one; not on a married woman even if she is ugly; and not on a woman's high-colored attire—the fine clothes she wears to enhance her charms. Whoever looks at a woman will in the end fall into transgression.[4]

It is no wonder that Jesus' disciples "marvelled" (John 4:27) when they found him speaking at the well with the woman from Samaria. Jesus was flagrantly ignoring social convention. He was also resisting a demeaning social convention. A woman was automatically classed as a threat to sexual continence, as an obstacle to male holiness, rather than as a being made in the image of God, a person capable of sharing all the gifts of personhood.

The convention was also counterproductive. The forbidden-fruit syndrome, recognized by Paul (Romans 7), refers to the phenomenon of the increased desire, which occurs when a flat prohibition is placed on the object of desire.

Jesus, of course, was not burdened by the forbidden-fruit syndrome or by any other syndrome. One syndrome undoubtedly associated with the prohibition against contact with women has not yet been mentioned, namely, "the-devil-made-me-do-it" syndrome. In Jewish literature the main reason for prohibiting contact with women was male weakness; yet the major blame for the fall of the male was placed on the female, a view aided by the Genesis story concerning Eve's "seduction" of Adam (Genesis 3:1-7). Unhappily, both men and women seem unable to shake "the-devil-made-me-do-it" syndrome, a syndrome which is rooted in sheer self-deception.

Naturally, Jesus would have nothing of self-deception. Indeed, he had no need to unload responsibility for sin on somebody else, for he was without sin. This fact should not lead us to think that unless and until we are spotless, we shall have to remain distant from the opposite sex. The way toward handling incontinent desire is to take full responsibility for it, not to attempt to evade or rationalize it. The sooner we admit that our heart is "deceitful above all things, and desperately corrupt" (Jeremiah 17:9), the sooner we will fly to the grace of God for forgiveness, cleansing, and power.

Returning now to Jesus' treatment of women, we find him crashing through the social conventions surrounding women. Not only did Jesus speak with women (see especially Luke 10:38-42), he also touched them constantly in his healing ministry and let them touch him.

Two incidents in the Gospels are particularly instructive examples of Jesus' loving relationships with women. The first concerns the woman with an issue of blood (probably hemorrhaging, Luke 8:40-48). She was, because of her bleeding, ritually unclean (Leviticus 15:25-28). Thus, those in the crowd who knew her would see her act—touching the hem of Jesus' garment—as a wicked act, for in touching Jesus she passed on her uncleanness to him. As the woman moved toward Jesus, we can see those horrified people trying to put as much distance between her and them as possible and whispering to others in the crowd to do the same. Yet Jesus reacted neither in horror nor revulsion but in compassion and comfort: "Daughter, your faith has made you well; go in peace."

The second incident concerns the woman "who was a sinner" (Luke 7:36-50). Jesus had been invited by a Pharisee to a dinner party. To the consternation of the Pharisee, the sinner-woman crashed his party. To his greater consternation she started doing all sorts of unseemly things to Jesus, such as shedding tears on his feet, kissing his feet, and drying his feet with her hair. Jesus' failure to shove the woman away in righteous indignation was a sure sign to the Pharisee that Jesus was not a prophet. Jesus' radical response to the woman was one of tenderness and compassion. After commending her actions to the Pharisee, Jesus declared her sins forgiven, sending her away with the words, "Go in peace."

Astonishing as Jesus' actions were in these incidents, they do not match his actions with regard to his band of traveling companions. Jesus included women in the band (Luke 8:1-3). What scandal—single women traveling with men in first-century Jewish society! Jesus simply tore up the book on conventions concerning women. In doing so, he set tongues wagging. We have little trouble reading between the lines of the criticism that Jesus was a friend of tax collectors and sinners (Matthew 11:19).

Lepers

Jesus did not merely crash through the barriers of convention which surrounded women; he also crashed through barriers surrounding other groups in Jewish society. One set of barriers he crashed through, perhaps the most formidable in Jewish society, was the set surrounding lepers.

In the Bible the term "leprosy" is used to cover a variety of skin diseases (mainly of the class psoriasis) and fungi (including mildew), as well as what we call leprosy, namely, Hansen's disease (Leviticus 13). Much of what was called "leprosy" then was not contagious or life-threatening but fairly innocuous. Yet the leper was "unclean."

This situation illustrates (for contemporary literalists) that the biblical laws of cleanliness have little or no systematic relation to the germ theory of disease. Note, for example, Jesus' remarks to the Pharisees about the washing of hands before eating (Mark 7:1-23). Jesus' disciples had not washed their hands; neither had Jesus told them to do so—failures which brought forth the criticism of the Pharisees. If the notions of clean and unclean find their rationale in the notions of health and disease, Jesus should have told his disciples to wash their hands. However, in not doing so, he showed emphatically that the issue was not one of health or disease but of religious condition. To be clean meant that a person was in a religious condition appropriate for participation in the religious activities of the Jewish community; to be unclean meant the reverse.

Whatever the full explanation of the clean and unclean, the lepers were the most unclean persons in Jewish society. As a result, the conventions applying to lepers were extremely harsh: they were to appear as if in mourning (clothes torn and hair uncombed); if anyone approached them, they were to cry out, "Unclean! Unclean!" so that everyone could avoid them; and they were to live apart from the community (Leviticus 13:45, 46). Lepers, then, were excluded from normal society and associations. They were untouchable, except by other lepers. Worse, they were viewed as objects of God's disfavor. According to rabbinical literature, leprosy was inflicted because of peculiarly grave sins.

Yet Jesus, disdaining rabbinic superstition, pulverized the barriers around lepers at the very outset of his ministry (Mark 1:40-45). We see a leper approaching Jesus. The man neither hesitates nor cries, "Unclean! Unclean!" but with a desperate determination steadily makes his way to Jesus. As for Jesus, he calmly awaits the leper, even invites him with his eyes. The leper, upon reaching Jesus, throws himself at Jesus' feet, imploring, "Lord, if you will, you can make me clean." But now . . . what is Jesus doing? he is TOUCHING the leper. Unbelievable! For how long had the leper been untouched, except by other lepers? For how long had he felt isolation and exclusion from family, friends, and normal society? For how long had he felt separated from God for sins which he "surely must have committed"? Yet Jesus touches him—a profound act—for it meant, "I welcome you back to the normal relations of society; I welcome you back to the company of God's people; I reassure you of the favor of God. You are clean!"

What a picture of Jesus—tender, sensitive, compassionate, and approachable. When persons and relationships are primary, a person welcomes all, even the worst outcasts. Approachability cannot be hidden; the approachable child of God is like a city on a hill, visible over the valley and for miles from the sky.

Tax Collectors

Another group that, in contrast to the lepers, moved about freely but was treated with scorn, hostility, and even hatred was the tax collectors. These people were the objects of such ill-will because they were the lackeys of Rome; moreover, they were the lackeys of Rome for material aggrandizement.

In its provinces Rome did not assign government officials to collect taxes. Instead, wealthy Romans bid for this privilege. They would contract to pay a certain amount to the treasury, putting up security to guarantee their word. They would then farm out the actual collecting to agents, whose remuneration was whatever monies they could collect over and above the sum due to the main contractor. The system obviously lent itself to gross abuse with the result that the term "tax collector" became synonymous with "dishonesty" and "extortion." Tax collectors had such a bad name that their money was not accepted for alms, nor would evidence from them be accepted in a court of law. Worst of all, though, they were in complicity with the hated Romans and were, therefore, in the eyes of the populace a low form of life.

Jesus saw tax collectors through different eyes. There is Matthew, for example, sitting at the toll house, engaging in his nefarious business (Matthew 9:9). But what is Jesus doing? He is going over to Matthew. Why? Of what can Jesus be thinking? He certainly has no goods to be taxed. Now he's talking to Matthew. What is he saying? Follow me? Jesus wants a tax collector to be one of his disciples? Impossible! What sort of man would associate with a tax collector?

Jesus is the perfect man, the man who acted as God meant for all men and women to act, with full appreciation of the value of persons and the value of relating lovingly to them. Jesus' enemies meant to heap abuse upon him by calling him the "friend of tax collectors" (Matthew 11:19). It is ironic that what Jesus' enemies saw as a defect, we see as a sign that "God was in Christ." Friendship, of course, is far from an easy matter, although the fashion these days is to use the term "friend" in a superficial way. True friendship, however, means much more than being acquainted with someone. Friendship means relating to and talking with Matthew; it means going to visit and eating dinner with Zacchaeus (Luke 19:1-10); it means sharing important slices of life with others; it means getting close to outcasts, even when social convention screams, "Stay away!" Yet staying away is the last thing an outcast needs.

What was wrong with the tax collector? His basic problem was that he was living for money. The only way to change him was to introduce him to a loving relationship. Jesus cut across the self-defeating exclusionary policies of his society by relating to the tax collector. And with what results! Matthew abandoned the toll house; Zacchaeus covenanted to give half of his goods to the poor, restoring four times what he owed to any whom he had defrauded. Anyone who has tasted the new wine of loving relationships will not be able to tolerate the old wine of selfishness.

Sinners

Another group of outcasts with whom Jesus associated was labelled "sinners." Jesus was not only the friend of tax collectors but also of sinners (Matthew 11:19). Who the term "sinners" included cannot be stated with certainty, but they were those who performed deeds generally recognized as sinful. The woman caught in the act of adultery was a sinner (John 8:2-10). Jesus, although treating her with the greatest tenderness, instructed her emphatically to go and sin no more. The One who came to bring men and women into loving relationships could not condone an act or lifestyle that substituted immediate, short-term pleasure for close, caring, loving relationships.

The term "sinner" probably also covered a host of others whose "sins" consisted essentially in failing to meet the niceties of rabbinic prescription. Jesus was considered a sinner because of the way he acted on the sabbath. He healed, instructed those he healed to "work" ("Pick up your pallet and walk!", John 5:8), permitted his disciples to pick ears of grain and rub them in their hands (Mark 2:23-28), did not instruct his disciples to wash before eating, nor did he wash (Luke 11:38), and so on. This behavior was contrary to rabbinic rules. The rules were, as a whole, the expression of a serious attempt to interpret divine law for specific situations and represent an earnestness of spirit, if not a sense of balance and proportion. Jesus behaved with consideration of the weightier matters of the law (Matthew 23:23) and of the two great commandments (Mark 12:28-34). The scribe who asked, "Which commandment is the first of all?" represented that sizable segment in the Jewish religious community that, like Jesus, sought to maintain a sense of proportion and priority. Indeed, the scribe was commended by Jesus, who said, "You are not far from the kingdom of God."

The church has often been afflicted with a loss of a sense of proportion and priority. It has legislated rules that have little or nothing to do with genuine religion, with relationship to God and others. The rules have run the gamut from how a person is to groom himself or herself to what a person is to drink. The rules do provide a specific measure of holiness, but a measure that is far easier to achieve than the measure of loving relationships. The rules are clear evidence that we simply do not seem to be able to grasp the grace of God. Rather than throwing ourselves on the tender mercies of God, we prefer to manufacture trivial, easily followed rules. It is much easier to fix one's hair in a certain way or abstain from some beverage or other or attend some church meeting regularly than to love God and others! Unfortunately, our easy rules succeed in bringing us a righteousness that is nothing more than filthy rags (Isaiah 64:6). A righteousness that is not rooted firmly in the grace of God and does not issue in a life committed to loving relationships is not the righteousness of the New Testament (Ephesians 2:8-10). Indeed, to adhere to human rules while neglecting the divine rule of loving relationships, or to give the same status to human rules as to the divine rule, is to engage in the sin of rebellion.

Teddy Roosevelt, when police commissioner of New York City, ran into a buzz saw of opposition over his efforts to enforce the Sunday closing law for taverns. A coalition of Protestant groups strongly supported him, but the German Lutherans, along with a number of secular groups, violently opposed him. And why not? Who would be so bold as to say that the German Lutherans would have been better Christians if they had refrained from drinking on Sunday? Such a judgment lacks biblical support.

The Bible does indicate that, whatever the sins of the sinners with whom Jesus associated, he was the target of a barrage of criticism. Here, for example, is Jesus at dinner in Matthew's house (Matthew 9:9-17):

> PHARISEE: Jesus, what are you doing eating with sinners? Don't you know that they are most likely unclean and that you, too, as a result of contact with them, will become unclean?
>
> JESUS: And don't you know that the sick need a physician? How can you fail to understand that no physician would ever do his job without contacting his patients. And whether you accept it or not, I am the physician come to heal the sick!

Jesus had come to bring persons back into relationship with God and with others. Yet how could he ever do so, how could he ever show sinners the priority of loving relationships if he was not willing to relate lovingly to them? True, he risked becoming ritually unclean, at least from the narrow rabbinic viewpoint; but then Jesus was also willing to risk the cross.

Conclusion

Jesus, as we have seen, shredded the conventions concerning the lowly, the despised, the outcast. His people have not always been quite so bold.

I frequent two places in my community regularly. At one place I associate with people who are, for the most part, of my race, class, and income. At the other place I associate with a more varied group—bankers, truck drivers, engineers, plumbers, white, black, hispanic, rich, poor, in-between. The first place is my church, which is hardly an aberration in the community. I do not know of a church which is not essentially homogeneous in terms of race and class. The other place is a cafe, run by my neighbor, a native Italian. How his cafe came to attract so heterogeneous a clientele in this southern town I do not know (apart from the natural friendliness of my neighbor). I only know that the cafe looks more as the church should than the churches in town do.

Sadly, my community is far from exceptional. A sociological study would reveal that most churches in North America adhere to the conventions of socioeconomic class and ethnic/racial background. There are silk-stocking churches, blue-collar churches, white churches, black churches, ethnic churches, and so on. The homogeneity of North American churches cannot be written off strictly to housing patterns. To be sure, persons with similar backgrounds tend to associate with one another, but we do not find churches in the New Testament structured after what people tend or have been conditioned to do.

We often hear that people who are not representative of the dominant group in a church would not feel comfortable there. Yet who ever said that the mission of the church is to make people feel comfortable? The further question is *why* people would not feel comfortable. Is the problem with the minority or with the majority group in the church?

The church that has its priorities straight—the church that sees loving relationships as central to its mission—is not going to let itself get caught in the uniformity trap. The imperative to relate lovingly to others cuts across every conventional barrier. If we relate only to those of our kind, if we never move beyond where we would naturally go, what evidence do we give of the new life of the Spirit? Anyone who has listened even casually to nonchurched persons knows that the church is usually seen as just another organization. One reason is that the composition of the church, with too few exceptions, parallels the composition of secular organizations. It is homogeneous. Obviously, if a church has trouble reaching out to persons of diverse backgrounds, it will also have trouble reaching out to the drug addict, the alcoholic, the felon, the prostitute.

A church that responded to the demands of Jesus would draw the response, "Hey, what's going on there?" As things stand, the response to the church is usually just a yawn. There is work to do! Jesus calls us to be inclusive, to break down the barriers of convention, to pursue loving relationships.

3

Jesus and the Affective Life
(Part One)

As the horse-drawn caisson bore the casket draped in Old Glory past the crowds of mourners, the television cameras focused on a figure dressed in black. She stood like a statue hewn from granite. Her jaw was set, her eyes fixed, her makeup flawless, unstained by any tear. She was the perfect stoic, a point repeatedly noted by the television announcer. "She bears herself well, with great courage." And so the remarks went about Jackie Kennedy on the day that her slain husband was buried at Arlington National Cemetery.

It is another scene; another time. The great warrior Achilles is weeping, crying out in unrestrained grief, pouring the dust of the ground over his head. Now he throws himself headlong upon the ground, tearing at his hair, sobbing, "Patroclus, my dearest comrade! You have fallen, fallen never to rise. You lie like a broken beast, your blood curdling the dust." An ear-piercing wail issues from his contorted lips. The face scarred from many battles is streaked with tears.

On the one hand, a refined woman, whose hands showed not even the slightest signs of coarse work, received approbation for being publicly unmoved over the death of her husband; on the other hand, a rough warrior, whose hands had often been stained with the blood of battle, openly and unashamedly mourned without the slightest hint of disapprobation from anybody. What we have here are two very different cultures. In Greek culture the expression of grief by the male was considered perfectly natural and normal. In our culture the expression of grief by the male is linked with weakness. If a man is to demonstrate his manliness, as well as courage and strength, he must suppress his grief, rise above it. Expression of grief by the female is accepted, if not commended, because "she is the weaker sex." The reason that Jackie Kennedy was commended is surely that she displayed "male" characteristics, especially valued in our culture, at least in 1963. It is interesting to note that the statements of approbation for Jackie Kennedy were, in the case of many commentators, the statements of males.

Expression of grief by men in our society has been considered inappropriate, being linked traditionally with characteristics viewed as feminine: sensitivity, emotionalism, weakness. Expressions of hostility, rage, and anger by the male have been considered perfectly appropriate. Thus, at various athletic events we are often treated to the spectacle of grown men engaging in fist fights (with fans cheering the combat on). Nobody seems to remember the proverb that "He who is slow to anger is better than the mighty, and he who rules his spirit than he who takes a city" (Proverbs 16:32).

What sort of expression of emotion or feeling* is appropriate for the children of the kingdom, for those who have sworn allegiance to a new culture? An adequate answer requires that we look once more to Jesus, the author and finisher of our faith.

---

*The terms "feeling" and "emotion" will be used interchangeably. If a distinction is present in our language, "feeling" is used for what is *experienced* or *felt*, "emotion" for what is *expressed*.

Emotions Expressed by Jesus

A brief review of the Gospel records indicates that Jesus expressed a wide range of emotions. He expressed wonder and amazement at the faith of the Roman centurion (Matthew 8:5-13); disappointment at the nine lepers who did not return to give thanks for healing (Luke 17:11-19) and at his disciples for going to sleep in his last hours (Mark 14:33-42); sorrow over the wickedness of Jerusalem (Luke 19:41-44) and at the tomb of his friend Lazarus (John 11:33-35); joy over the success of a mission of the disciples, as well as over the purposes of God (Luke 10:21); compassion for the multitudes (Matthew 9:36-38); and love, including special love (John 13:1, 23; Mark 10:17-22).

"Positive" and "Negative" Emotions

Given the emotions that Jesus had and expressed, as well as those Scripture does not address, how may we sort them out? The emotions do not divide neatly; however, we might make a division into "positive" and "negative" emotions. We do view emotions positively and negatively, although they are not, in and of themselves, good or bad. We approve unhesitatingly of love, joy, and sympathy; we see them as worthy of expression, as healthy and good. Other emotions, such as hatred, anger, and fear, we tend to disapprove; we do not wish to have them or we think they ought to be suppressed, eliminated, or expressed only reservedly and under special circumstances.

The division is arbitrary but it provides a ready classification for study. So we shall use these categories.

The Expression of Emotion

Our capacity to feel is a natural one. We are affective beings, beings with emotional capacities. Thus, we might conclude that just as our capacity to reason is to be expressed and exercised, so our capacity to feel or emote is to be expressed and exercised. We fear the emotionless, "ice cube" character. We associate such a person with the professional killer, the undercover agent, the terrorist. Even the ancient stoics, with their admirable qualities, leave *us* cold because *they* were cold. The stoic objective was perfect equanimity of mind, a state that can be reached only by turning off the emotions. Listen, for example, to the words of Epictetus.

> When you see a person weeping in sorrow either when a child goes abroad or when he is dead, or when the man has lost his property, take care that the appearance does not hurry you away with it, as if he were suffering in external things. But straightway make a distinction in your own mind, and be in readiness to say, it is not that which has happened that afflicts this man, for it does not afflict another, but it is the opinion about this thing which afflicts the man. So far as words then do not be unwilling to show him sympathy, and even if it happens so, to lament with him. But take care that you do not lament internally also.[1]

The stoic was after a tranquil flow of life, freedom from perturbation and vexation, indifference. But such a life kills feelings that are an essential aspect of our humanity. The classical Greek thinkers showed a healthy respect for the affective life, advocating not killing or suppressing emotions but controlling and guiding them by reason. We cannot, then, by happy with suppressed emotion.

Neither, though, can we be happy with the unrestrained expression of emotion. Some followers of the Freudian understanding of the self have reasoned that since the repression of emotion is bad (banishing emotions to the unconscious only guarantees that they will return in a supercharged form to haunt and harass us), the expression of emotion is good. Therefore, persons should "let it all hang out." Freud, of course, never endorsed such an idea; neither has anyone else who has given much attention to the issue. Just as we do not endorse every expression of reason (for example, the Nazi use of reason to develop a system to eliminate Jews and to experiment with humans), so we have little justification to endorse every expression of emotion.

"Negative" Emotions
Grief

Jesus said, "Blessed are those who mourn, for they shall be comforted" (Matthew 5:4). This statement demonstrates the conflict between the values of our culture and the values of Jesus, for grief has been viewed in our culture as a sign of weakness, something to be suppressed by the strong person. Yet Jesus did not say, "Blessed are the weak when they mourn." He said, "Blessed are those who mourn" or, "Blessed are you that weep now, for you shall laugh" (Luke 6:21). Generally, grief is experienced in relation to tragedy, loss, frustration, or failure. But what about loss, frustration, and failure that are inconsequential in terms of kingdom values—such as a substantial loss in gold futures or failure to win a community service award or an important race? The words of Jesus may still apply. Even in inconsequential cases mourning may bring some comfort, for the point of Jesus is twofold: (1) our feelings about loss or failure need to be recognized (admitted) and expressed; and (2) doing so normally results in the amelioration of grief. Those who jam the lid on their grief are headed for trouble.

So are those who mourn excessively over inconsequentials. A person cannot, for example, ignore Jesus' words about mammon and seeking God's kingdom first and then expect the special working of God to deal with any resulting grief. We can expect, in inconsequential matters, the benefits of recognizing and expressing grief, but we cannot expect to be "blessed" (a word which includes the promise of the special activity of God). Grieving over inconsequentials may be the means that drives one to a reexamination of values. This reexamination is really the only cure for unnecessary grief over loss or failure. It may be disappointing to lose money or to lose an important race but neither event is worth brooding over for any period of time. Jesus did not say, "Blessed are those who weep now" to those who weep over inconsequential matters.

To what mourners, then, did Jesus refer? One way to answer this question is to examine the mourning of Jesus. He wept over Jerusalem—over its abysmal record of response to God's love and faithfulness, over its failure to enter into the fullness of God's blessings, over its past destruction and deportation, and over its coming destruction. Jesus wept, in effect, over the tragedy of God's people, a tragedy of willful rebellion. But he also wept at Lazarus's tomb. There he wept as he saw Mary and her friends weeping (John 11:33-35). Here is a case of Jesus grieving in identification with others, of "weeping with those who weep." To be sure, Jesus could see that the death of Lazarus was not a tragedy for it was to be a mighty victory. However, he was sensitive to the perspective of others who could see only tragedy. Perhaps Jesus also grieved over the tragedy he saw ahead. He knew death would wreak incomparable havoc on the human scene until death was finally swallowed up in victory. So he wept.

Another way of discovering the meaning of Jesus' words "Blessed are those who weep now" is to look at the Old Testament. Over what do God's people sorrow? They mourned death; thus, David wept over the death of Jonathan (2 Samuel 1:11-27). They also grieved over sin, thus David sorrowed for his adultery and murder (Psalms 32 and 51). In addition, the psalmist grieves over the loss of the sense of God's presence and action (Psalms 42; 69; 119:81-88). Death, sin, and the loss of the sense of God's presence and action are worthy of grief. To grieve over a sensed loss of God's presence and action is to step toward experiencing again that presence and action; to grieve over sin is to step toward forgiveness; and to grieve over death is to step toward wholeness and healing.

I have a friend whose wife died tragically while she was still in her twenties. He was devastated, and not in the least reluctant to show his devastation. He told me that the custom of his Jewish community was to mourn for a year. There is great wisdom in that custom, for to mourn is to keep the feelings that go with death—grief, anger, confusion, guilt, and many more—on the conscious level, where they can be handled far better than in the darkness of what we generally call the "unconscious." In addition, to mourn is to let others know that we are approachable. To cope with grief, we must have the warmth and affection of others; however, we shall never get that warmth and affection if we do not appear to need it. Further, to mourn for a year is to say that with the deep grief associated with great loss, nothing other than time will work. There are no quick-fix therapies. There is only time. Somehow, after six months, after a year, after two years the hurt is not as acute. Indeed, if relationships were positive, the hurt is ultimately transformed into cherished memories. Finally, to mourn for a year, a limited time, is to say that life goes on; it must go on. Thus, we are to get back to the business of living, to reconstructing life, to filling the void.

In sum, grief must be recognized and expressed whatever our culture may say to the contrary. To put the lid on it is to ask for trouble, to block off the natural healing process, the support of friends and loved ones, and the grace of God.

Anger

The church has traditionally been uncomfortable with anger. Numerous religious books emphasizing personal holiness look with disfavor even on irritability, appealing to passages such as 1 Corinthians 13:5 for authority.

Many psychologists see anger as perfectly natural but note that it is normally not useful. They believe anger is rooted in frustration and maintain that the original cause of frustration is often forgotten or submerged in consciousness and anger then generalizes to other objects (persons). Anger that is not directed properly is both inappropriate and ineffective. Yet, say the psychologists, even if expressed properly, anger usually does little good, exacerbating rather than ameliorating frustration.

Whatever the church or psychologists say about anger, we know that Jesus became angry. In Mark 3:1-6 we read of Jesus' anger toward his opponents in the religious establishment, "He looked around at them with anger." His scathing denunciation of the scribes and Pharisees, for example (Matthew 23), can only be seen as an expression of anger. The same is true for his expulsion of the merchants from the temple. In addition, Jesus became vexed with his disciples because of their obtuseness (Mark 4:10-13; 7:17-19; 8:13-21); he also became vexed with the people (Mark 9:19).

Thus, those in the church who maintain that love is inconsistent with anger ignore clear biblical teaching. It is necessary to remember that the culture of the church (the traditions and values passed from one generation to another) is often not in line with the culture of the kingdom. As noted previously, the church in general and individual denominations in particular have developed numerous traditions that have little relation to clear biblical teaching or the example of Jesus. Jesus got angry.

Instead of trying to rationalize away the anger of Jesus, it may be helpful to try to understand it. To begin, though, we will note the approach that many psychologists take toward anger, as well as toward other supposedly negative emotions. Their main contention is that emotions must be recognized. Thus, just as the person who denies grief is headed for trouble, so is the person who denies anger. In fact, to deny one's anger is simply to fall prey to the old nemesis of self-deception. Nobody is ever going to live abundantly, as long as he or she is weighted with self-deception. Surely when Jesus said, "Let your yes be yes and your no, no" (Matthew 5:37), he was speaking about self-honesty, as well as honesty toward others.

Granting that anger is to be recognized, what are the moral proprieties of having and expressing anger? Strictly speaking, the moral issues are concerned with the latter.

In other words, an emotion of any sort is not right or wrong, for only actions are right or wrong. Yet insofar as emotions influence actions, we should certainly extend moral concern to them. We might refer to certain emotions as morally good or bad, just as we refer to motives as morally good or bad. Perhaps, though, the labeling of emotions as morally good or bad should be avoided. Putting a moral label on emotions tends only to obscure understanding—understanding the causes of emotions as well as the effects.

The question is whether getting angry, showing anger, or acting in anger is justifiable. Jesus did all three. What shall we say about him? First of all, we must observe that Jesus did not go around angry. If he did, we could never believe a word he said about granting us his peace, for the angry soul is not a peaceful soul. Indeed, the angry soul is a troubled soul, a stormy sea. The continually angry person will likely have not only a disturbed inner life but physical and relational problems as well.

Sylvia had landed a job as a legal secretary after looking for over a month. She was competent in her work but had trouble relating to others. In other jobs she had been known to snap at clients for no apparent reason. In her new position Sylvia would be doing research and thus would have to relate, essentially, just to the attorneys. Of course, she had been known to lash out at her "bosses"; in fact, she had lost her last position because of an outburst at the senior partner of the firm.

Yet outbursts were not Sylvia's only problem. Her attendance record was poor. After outbursts at the office she would inevitably be unable to sleep. So she would take a sleeping pill and simply not wake up in time for work. Actually, she was having to rely more and more on sedatives, even though she was only twenty-six years old. The pills provided temporary relief from stress but did not touch the deeper physical problem of stomach ulcers, a problem that had appeared in her sophomore year in high school and had contributed to her poor attendance record.

To be sure, Sylvia had reason to be angry. Her early life had been one of parental neglect and abuse. She had run away from home several times and had been beaten by her father for doing so. Sylvia had separated herself from her parents, yet the break had seemed to aggravate her anger.

To evaluate Sylvia in moral terms—to say that her treatment of people was wrong or that her anger was morally bad—seems pointless. We would rather say that she was an unfortunate young woman, that she had never been given a chance to start life properly. Yet a belief in human freedom will not allow this analysis. If we can be held responsible by God and our fellow human beings, if our actions make a difference in history, if we can be commanded to repent—all notions firmly enshrined in the Bible—then we must be free. We are not like straws in the air, tossed about by the prevailing winds. Rather, we have genuine choice; we have the freedom of indeterminism— that is, whatever we choose, we could have chosen differently.

Mark hardly remembered his father, who had been killed in an industrial accident when Mark was only three. Mark's mother remarried when he was six and began a lifestyle of bar-hopping practically every evening of the week. Mark was either left with a babysitter or simply put to bed early. If he ever complained or expressed fear of staying by himself, his stepfather reprimanded him with a slap across the face. In fact, his stepfather abused both Mark and his mother. The marriage was stormy but lasted until Mark's senior year in high school. During high school Mark had little opportunity for social activities because he was, and had been for years, the official babysitter for his younger sister.

In spite of his home life, Mark was remarkably cheerful. He got along with just about everybody. The senior yearbook listed him as "Mr. Congeniality." As for his attitude toward his mother and stepfather, he looked on them more with pity than anything else. He simply was not angry with them. Of course he did not appreciate the slaps across the face; neither did he appreciate having to babysit with his sister every night. Yet when he left home immediately after graduation, he did not leave with bitterness, making a great scene with his mother. He left with a sort of heaviness, a grief—for his mother had taken up the company of another man similar to Mark's stepfather.

Mark's story contradicts the theory of early life as the singular influence in personality development, a theory which found one of its strongest opponents in the French existentialist writer Jean Paul Sartre. Sartre denies that we are just products of our environment. What shapes and determines our direction in life are our *free* responses to the conditions in which we find ourselves. His thesis would be that Sylvia and Mark freely chose—perhaps not with full, considered awareness but chose nonetheless—to respond to their parents as they did. To deny responsibility—to blame parents—would be to deny freedom, a denial that Sartre says is nothing less than self-deception.

Sartre's position is hardly without controversy, but it is at least as consistent with biblical teaching as the view that human action is strictly determined; that is, humans cannot choose other than what they actually choose. Their choices are entirely the consequence of physical makeup, environment, or the activity of God.

Whatever we may say about responsibility, we may surely say, in the case of Sylvia, that anger is devouring her. Moreover, whatever we think about her ability to reverse course, we may also surely say that she needs to do so. (Note: to believe in her freedom is not necessarily to believe that she does not need help.) Regardless of the moral status of her anger, it is useless and harmful both to herself and others. The harm to herself is not just psychological but physical.

The question with which we began, though, and the

question to which we must return is that of Jesus' anger. What shall we say about it from both a moral and a practical standpoint? First of all, we need to look more closely at the situations in which Jesus became angry.

In Mark 3:1-6 Jesus became angry with the religious leaders because they questioned the healing of a man on the sabbath. Essentially, these people were out to get Jesus because he threatened their position and power. They viewed themselves as highly religious and moral and therefore could not admit they were persecuting Jesus just because he threatened their status. In other words, they were grossly self-deceived—Jesus called them hypocrites—in using a religious rule to justify their intentions. What they used was the accusation of sabbath violation. The accusation revealed an imperviousness to plain moral and religious truth. Thus, Jesus asked his accusers, "Is it allowable to do people good on the sabbath, or to do them harm? To save life or kill?" (v. 4). His accusers make no answer, possibly out of embarrassment. They certainly should have been embarrassed to have such questions directed at them, questions that would need to be raised only for the morally obtuse. Probably, though, his accusers made no answer because they had been unmasked in public; their self-deception was made plain. In silent rage they stormed out of the synagogue and held a meeting to see how they might put Jesus, their unmasker, to death.

Jesus, then, became angry with self-deception, with self-deceivers who obscured fundamental moral and religious truths. Jesus' denunciation in Matthew 23 spelled out the moral/religious fog in which a sizable segment of the religious leadership had placed itself.

The cleansing of the temple is another case involving self-deception and moral/religious fog. Those who sold animals and exchanged money in the temple were out for a quick buck and, in some cases, a not-too-honest buck. Yet these merchants undoubtedly viewed themselves as both benign and useful, since they provided an essential service to the weary traveler. There was no need to bring a sheep or crate of pigeons from Capernaum. Just plunk down the required amount for an animal appropriate for passover or temple sacrifice. Also, for a fee, the appropriate half-shekel pieces for the annual temple tax could be obtained from the money changers. One had to expect a little price gouging in this exchange, but then business was business.

Yes, and the house of God was the house of God—meant for contact with the "Holy One of Israel." To consider crass materialism consistent with the purposes of the temple was to be in gross self-deception, as was to think that the shouting, the bleating of sheep, and the general hubbub surrounding the pilgrims suitably prepared them for prayer and worship. So Jesus drove out the whole crew in the hope of dislodging some of the self-deception.

Here, perhaps, is a clue for understanding Jesus' expression of anger. His anger was not a mere case of play-acting. The biblical narrative portrays the anger of Jesus as genuine. However, the issue now is function. What was the function of Jesus' anger? What effects were likely to follow? One answer is that the strong expression of anger has a shock effect, especially when displayed by someone who does not display it often. Jesus' display of anger in the temple was like hitting the merchants over the head, saying, "Open your eyes!"

Flannery O'Connor's "Revelation" illustrates that anger can be effective, even when expressed without benevolent intent.[2] Mrs. Turpin, the main character, is forced to see herself as she is—a bigoted woman—by a girl who angrily throws a book at Mrs. Turpin, calling her an old warthog.

Of course, anger is often effective not only with those who are the objects of anger but also with the person who becomes angry. Anger is a considerable stimulus to action. Jesus became angry and tossed the religious frauds out of the temple. We might become angry over the neglect of the poor and get moving to correct the situation.

Some anger, then, is functional. More importantly, though, anger seems as appropriate in some situations as laughter is in others. Indeed, we might even hold in moral disapproval the person who looks with cool equanimity on willful ignorance, self-deception, intellectual laziness, selfishness, injustice, cruelty, and so on. What would we think, for example, of a person who with perfect calm viewed films of the horrors of Auschwitz or read Eli Wiesel's *Night*? The Bible gives us little reason to conclude that anger is never appropriate. To think of the thundering Old Testament prophets expressing anything but "the rage of the Lord" is to think of beings in an artifical, antiseptic environment but not of persons immersed in the events of Hebrew history.

Thus, we may make at least two claims about anger: (1) it is appropriate, even called for, in some situations; (2) it is very effective in some situations. The qualifying phrase "some situations" is all-important. The problem with Sylvia, for example, was that she expressed her anger in the wrong situations. To have been angry at her parents at some point (or points) of her life for their neglect and abuse would have been perfectly appropriate; but to harbor her anger into and throughout her adult life was inappropriate, ineffective, and detrimental.

The deeper issue here is one of personal relations. How can anger affect personal relations positively? Part of the answer is that action that appropriately calls forth anger is likely to be action that is already hindering personal relations—selfishness, injustice, cruelty, and so on. Obviously, we would not be interested in having a close relationship with a person who was cruel, selfish, self-deceptive, or exploitive. Insofar as anger is effective in bringing about a change, in removing the attitudes and forms of behavior that impair and block closeness, it clears the way for the development of loving relationships.

Jean simply exploded. She had taken all she could. She had worked for years on her degree and had been looking forward to graduation ceremonies. Since the completion of her degree, she and her husband, Arnold, had moved to another state. Yet graduation was important to her, and if they flew, Arnold would have to miss only a day of work. He had promised to go with her but had started manufacturing excuses over the last month: they couldn't afford the loss of a day's wage; the trip for two was just too expensive; he was afraid of flying; and so on. Finally, on the Friday before the trip, Arnold just said flatly that he wasn't going. What really seemed to be at issue was Arnold's Friday evening card game; he'd have to miss it.

Jean blew up. She ticked off the whole list of Arnold's thoughtless, self-centered actions—and the list was long. She was through being his slave, jumping through his hoop. She would go to her graduation by herself, but he better be prepared for a divorce.

Arnold had never really heard his wife talk like this—a real tirade, uncommon for Jean's churchly mouth. Of course Arnold had never really *heard* his wife. In any case, he was shocked. He did everything to get her to quiet down except to say that he would go to her graduation.

On the Saturday when she was gone he began to think about Jean and her threat to leave him. He had tried to brush off her outburst during the week, but it just didn't brush off. His wife had never acted like that. Now he began to see what a self-centered soul he was. He did not change his behavior that Saturday, but he did start a long journey, a journey involving professional counseling with his wife, a journey that transformed Arnold considerably. Eventually he ceased being an exploiter and became a sharer.

The Arnold stories may be few and far between, but any stories of fundamental character change are few and far between. Still, anger can serve to focus on the obstacles to relationship in such a way that the obstacles finally get removed.

In addition to being effective sometimes, anger has the consistent function of demonstrating our essential humanity. Humans are emotional creatures; thus, to have and to express emotions is to emphasize our humanity. Indeed, to express feelings and emotions *appropriately* is to demonstrate our humanity most emphatically, for appropriate expression reveals the exercise of reason as well as moral judgment. What does this point have to do with personal relationships?—a great deal. We relate to those who strike us as human. The person without emotions (Mr. or Ms. Ice Cube) simply turns us off. We want to relate to a real person, a flesh and blood feeling and emoting human being, not a machine. We want to be around a being who responds to the full scope of our humanity, a scope that includes our affective life.

The scope of our humanity also includes our rational and moral life. Thus, we are not interested in someone who indiscriminately emotes—animals do that; however, animals are surely far removed from what will satisfy us. (The beautiful story in Genesis 2 is instructive. God created the animals in order to fill the void in Adam, in order to provide him with companions, in order to remove his loneliness. Yet after Adam saw all the animals and named them, he was as lonely as ever. No true companion had been provided for him. He needed a being of like nature to his, a being with feelings and emotions but also with reason and moral judgment. He needed Eve.)

In addition to demonstrating our humanity, the appropriate expression of anger demonstrates our honesty, which is also essential for loving relationships. To be sure, the inappropriate expression of anger demonstrates honesty no less than the appropriate expression of anger. (Sylvia was honest enough, but her relationships suffered terribly because her anger was inappropriately expressed.) Sheer honesty in expressing anger is hardly adequate; honesty needs to be linked with appropriate expression of anger.

Finally, the appropriate expression of anger demonstrates genuine care—care about a person or what a person is doing. When we don't care, we say, "So what?" Anger is never a "so what?" type of response. Insofar as anger expresses caring for persons, it is helpful in establishing loving relationships.

The extensive concentration on the emotion of anger is useful in that some lessons apply to other feelings or emotions. First, expressing emotion may be an expression of caring. Second, expressing emotion is a form of honesty that may be helpful to relationships, depending on whether the emotions are appropriately expressed. Third, and connected with the point on honesty, is that emotions must be recognized; to deny our emotions is to fall into self-deception. Fourth, appropriately expressing emotions demonstrates our essential humanity, our nature as beings made in the image of God. If we are made in the image of God, we may infer that in some sense God also has emotions. This inference is fully supported by biblical literature—God loves as a parent, grieves over sin, becomes angry, and so on. Fifth, appropriately expressing emotions is functional. The exact function depends on the particular emotion as well as on the situation. Finally, expressing an emotion may be appropriate or inappropriate. The exact situations in which each emotion is appropriate cannot be spelled out in detail. Moreover, emotional issues are complicated by cultural criteria for what is appropriate. Yet some criteria definitely rise above culture. Anybody who expressed grief over a stroke of good fortune or humor over the death of a close friend would surely be viewed as engaging in inappropriate behavior. By the same token, laughing at grief or death is clearly inappropriate. Even if, for example, humor was expressed in the face of death, that humor would probably be a cloak for grief, or a diversion from grief, or a transformation of grief, the assumption being that grief is what is appropriate, regardless of culture.

Hatred

Although anger is an appropriate and useful emotion in

certain circumstances, not all of the "negative" emotions function similiarly. Hatred, for one, is dissimilar. First and foremost, we do not find hatred in the repertoire of Jesus' emotions—and with good reason. Hatred is plainly and simply a destructive emotion. It is unfettered hostility, single-minded animosity, malignant ill will, delight in or desire to see or bring about harm to another. Hatred may have many degrees, but at bottom it is, according to Nat Turner, "so . . . obdurate that no sympathy, no human warmth, no flicker of compassion can make the faintest nick or scratch upon the stony surface of its being."[3]

To be sure, hatred may not be without reason, any more than anger. Recently the papers carried the story of a father in Louisiana who killed the abductor of his young son as the abductor was being escorted by authorities from a plane. The father suspected the man not only of abducting his son but also of molesting him sexually. Thus, the father had reason for his hatred; yet the reason did not justify the action taken. However, hatred hardly looks for justification; or if it does, it finds whatever justification it wants. Hatred is not reasonable; it is an enflaming passion.

Dale and A. J., twin brothers, had a violent falling out over their oil drilling business. Dale accused A. J. of trying to edge him out of the business. Harsh words turned into shoving and then fists flew. The brawl, which destroyed the business office, terminated only with the intervention of the police. Since that bloody brawl, the brothers, who live within blocks of one another, have not spoken, except through their lawyers, for thirty years. Neither one has made the slightest move toward reconciliation, even though their wives have urged them to do so. Both remain bitter, hostile, and unforgiving, each one continually dreaming up new ways to harass and hurt the other.

Hating is simply useless. If the one who hates does not destroy the object of hatred, he or she will seek to do as much harm as possible and never seek reconciliation. Hatred is therefore destructive of relationships.

Of course, the person who hates is likely to say, "Well, I just can't help it. If she'd done to you what she did to me, you'd hate her, too." Perhaps, but the notion that we cannot do anything about our feelings is one of the great myths of our culture. We may not be able to change our feelings on demand, any more than we can shed ten pounds by wishing; but we can change our feelings, just as we can shed ten pounds. In both cases, we must map out and commit ourselves to a disciplined program of change; moreover, the program for the change of feelings will probably be lengthier and more difficult than the program for weight reduction. Yet change of feelings can be accomplished. The power of God is surely nothing if it is insufficient to effect a change of destructive feelings. The New Testament is unambiguous about the capacity of God's power to change us from hating to loving persons. Anybody, Christian or not, can normally effect a change of feelings. The issue for the non-Christian may be the lack of motivation to change. As for the Christian, we might say that God's power is most obviously expressed in new motivation to change.

Dislike

Few people like to admit genuinely hating someone. We do not hate; we just dislike. Perhaps, but perhaps we are just deceiving ourselves. (Dislike can easily slide into hatred. It is important to be aware of this phenomenon if we are to rid ourselves of hate.)

Yet some people we may not genuinely hate; all the same, we may dislike them or, less strongly, just not like them. It appears that Jesus did not like the religious leaders he denounced so vigorously. Of course, Jesus seemed to like some of the leaders; at least he went to the homes of a number of them for dinner. However, those who were parading their religiosity and exploiting the people could hardly be considered people whom Jesus liked.

The fact is that some people have qualities that simply

make them unlikable. Arnold, for example, was extremely self-centered, so self-centered that we could wonder how Jean even liked him. Self-centered people are difficult to be around. They corner the conversation, concentrating strictly on their own agenda; they are insensitive; they are exploitive; they are boorish; they are a pain! We do not wish them ill; neither do we try to harm them; indeed, we hope that they change and may even try to get them to change. Yet failing change, they are not the sort of people we want to be around. We cannot relate to them. Having a close relationship with someone who is not sensitive or caring is simply impossible.

Guilt and Fear

Although Jesus had a substantial repertoire of feelings and emotions, there were some he apparently did not have. Jesus did not feel guilt; neither did he seem to feel fear, except perhaps in the Garden of Gethsemane. A careful analysis of the biblical passages concerning the garden scene is beyond the scope of this study. However, the idea that Jesus experienced fear in Gethsemane seems consistent with his humanity, with the fact that he, too, had to live by faith and had to struggle with doubt and fear. Looking at Jesus, we can conclude that fear is a natural and appropriate emotion in many circumstances.

There was recently a television segment on a lifesaving program of the U.S. Coast Guard. The program involves training in special powerboats in rough surf close to a rocky shore. A captain, a veteran of thirty years, was asked by a reporter whether he was ever afraid. "You bet I am," he said. "If I ever lost my fear, I wouldn't last a minute in these waters." Although Jesus calmed the storm on the Sea of Galilee and usually seemed to be without fear (Mark 4:35-41), we can hardly expect to be fearless, even on an irregular basis. The New Testament indicates clearly that the miracles surrounding Jesus were exceptional, associated with the exceptional nature of his revelation (Hebrews

1:1-2; 2:1-4). In other words, we cannot expect divine deliverance in every crisis of our lives.

Of course, to be fearful about everything which may or may not happen is no more to be commended than is to be angry continually. At any rate, whether our fear is appropriate or not, we need to keep it out in the open (a truth we have learned about emotions in general). To shove fear into the closet is self-deception and makes the constructive handling of fear difficult, if not impossible. To keep fear on the conscious level, particularly when fear is appropriate, is to be motivated to be cautious or to escape or to eliminate the circumstances causing the fear.

Fear, like the other emotions, has its degrees, sliding at one end of the scale into anxiety. No special remarks are necessary for anxiety, except that Jesus noted our anxiety over the wrong things, our material pursuits (Matthew 6:25-34). Paul notes his anxiety over the churches (1 Corinthians 11:28), an anxiety which we would have to say is perfectly appropriate. Some things are worth being anxious about.

Along with fear and the other "negative" emotions, guilt needs to be kept out of the closet. We have noted briefly that one of the things worth grieving about is our sin. Grieving over our sin requires, naturally enough, recognizing our sin. The final step to comfort and healing is forsaking our sin. The writer of Proverbs puts both steps together when he says, "He who conceals his transgressions will not prosper, but he who confesses and forsakes them will obtain mercy" (Proverbs 28:13).

Yet much guilt is improper. Psychologists have, in fact, talked about neurotic guilt, guilt over that about which we should not feel guilty.

Charles rushed out of the house. He was, as usual, getting off to work late. He hopped into the car, slammed it into reverse, and started backing out of the driveway when—a scream! He had run over his twenty-month old daughter. But how was that possible? She was in the house!

Tragically, she was not, for she had toddled outside and started playing under the car.

Charles yelled for his wife, who ran out, scooped up the crushed child with a low moan and, sobbing, sat down next to Charles, who roared out of the driveway and raced to the emergency room. After three hours of surgery the doctor appeared in the waiting room. Their daughter was dead.

The burden was too great to bear. Charles expunged the whole incident from his consciousness. He had not run over Christi. She was, in his mind, off visiting her grandparents.

Charles was feeling guilt over his finitude—over his inability to play God, to be omniscient. We can take precautions against mistakes and accidents, but we are unlikely to avoid them altogether. Moreover, when they occur, playing the "if-I-had-only" game is useless and devastating, particularly if we acted reasonably to begin with. Charles, for example, had no reason to believe that his daughter was under the car. How she got out of the house was never explained satisfactorily. He never checked under his car. Why should he? Christi was either in the house or in the fenced backyard. So should he be distraught, devastated? Absolutely. But guilty? Never. Indeed, even when we have not acted reasonably and prudently, guilt is of value only to the extent that it produces change. Chronic guilt is as useless and harmful as chronic anger or fear.

Yet the story of improper guilt is not finished. We could tell about the guilt, for example, that is a result of failure to live up to parental demands, often improper parental demands—such as the demand to pursue a career goal one of the parents failed to achieve. There is also the story of guilt arising from the improper standards imposed by many churches. Those brought up in the church have often been burdened with a load of dos and don'ts that have little to do with New Testament demands. In the film "Chariots of Fire" we met a Scottish Presbyterian athlete, brought up to treat the Christian Lord's Day as the Jewish sabbath. Indeed, he referred to the Lord's Day as the sabbath. The result was susceptibility to guilt over a whole list of forbidden sabbath activities, activities which in many cases had little relevance to the Christian observance of the Lord's Day.

Unfortunately, the church has had a great capacity for cranking out irrelevant prescriptions for holy living, with some churches pushing prescriptions diametrically opposed to those of other churches. Some churches forbid dancing; others have dances at the church. Some church camps forbid the mixing of sexes while swimming; others never thought of having anything but "mixed" swimming. Some churches forbid the use of alcohol; others provide it at church functions. Some churches demand tithing, forbidding the use of bazaars or other money-raising activities; others rely mainly on money-raising activities from bazaars to bingo. And so we could go on. The person raised in the culture of a particular church will feel guilty about what is said to be a sin. Too often the stress placed on the nonessential is far greater than the stress placed on the essential of loving relationships. Thus, a woman who wears makeup may be far more the target of church criticism than a woman who continually uses other people for her own gain, including the members of her own family. Naturally, that which is stressed most will bring the strongest pangs of guilt. Far too many raised in the church today are walking around with burdens of guilt which they simply need to unload. We have too much proper guilt to handle—guilt over botched relationships—to carry about the additional load of improper guilt, guilt that invariably diverts us from the main issue.

Proper guilt, then, is feeling guilty about what we ought to feel guilty about—failure to adhere to the ideals of self-growth and loving relationships. Unfortunately, just as culture can condition us to feel guilty about the wrong things, so it can condition us to feel no guilt whatsoever about the right things. For example, success, the great god of our society, is hardly identical with being a caring person or one who is on a religious search. Thus, a person conditioned to pursue success without restraint may not have the slightest twinge of conscience about using, abusing, and being uncaring about others—or about totally neglecting the pursuit of God. To get people of this mindset to reorder their values with respect to relationships or even to reflect on the matter is one of the very difficult tasks of the church.

For those who do experience proper guilt, a twofold process of forgiveness is necessary: forgiveness of self and forgiveness from God. In both cases a genuine turning from our waywardness is required, along with a commitment to kingdom values.

Self-forgiveness calls for special comment. A strongly ingrained idea in our culture (our penal system runs on the idea) is that we must pay for our sins, our crimes, our misdeeds. How, then, can we so cheaply be let off the guilt-hook as Christianity proposes we can be? How can a word of divine forgiveness dissolve our guilt? Surely, we must have gotten it wrong. We have to do something; we have to flagellate ourselves in some way. Although, when we have broken a relationship, all we really need to hear is that the other has accepted us on the basis of our genuine sorrow over having broken the relationship. Our sorrow is a way of saying, "I commit myself to avoid weakening or breaking relationships; I commit myself anew to pursuing relationships, in particular, the relationship with you." That exchange amounts to forgiveness.

Unfortunately, accepting divine forgiveness or the forgiveness of others will just never happen unless we forgive ourselves. Moreover, in a case such as that of Charles, forgiving ourselves is severely complicated by the fact that the guilt is kept in the dark waters of the self. Indeed, the complications are twofold, perhaps threefold: the guilt is improper; it is shielded from the penetrating beams of consciousness; and it might be nurtured by a weak sense of self-worth. Under these conditions, especially a combination of them, we can ask for forgiveness a hundred times a day without ever feeling forgiven. In fact, our guilt might even increase.

The basic lesson we must learn is that fundamental to experiencing release from guilt is either the recognition and emotional acceptance of the impropriety of our guilt or self-forgiveness. As for self-forgiveness, to fail to forgive ourselves is in effect to fail to accept forgiveness from God or others. We are saying, "I am unworthy of forgiveness; I must make myself worthy before I can truly be forgiven." The problem with people who think like this is that they are unlikely ever to make themselves worthy enough for forgiveness. How to bring people to accept themselves and the forgiveness freely offered by a loving God or by loving people is one of the great tasks of the church. It is not an easily accomplished task. Sometimes professional counseling will be required to bring about self-acceptance. Always, the consistent, persistent demonstration of forgiving acceptance in the concrete interpersonal relationships of the church is required.

4

Jesus and the Affective Life
(Part Two)

The previous chapter focused on feelings and emotions we chose to call negative. This chapter will focus on the positive feelings and emotions expressed by Jesus. "Positive" emotions are defined here as those generally approved or perceived as evidencing strength, growth, maturity, or success.

Love

Naturally, the first positive emotion we think of when we think of Jesus is love (along with emotions associated with love such as compassion and sympathy). Perhaps we can work our way into the subject by exploring what appears to be Jesus' special love for certain persons.

Mark reports that Jesus looked on the rich young ruler and loved him (Mark 11:15), a statement not used in referring to others whom Jesus called to follow him. Jesus is also said to have loved Martha, Mary, and Lazarus (John 11:5), again a qualifying statement not used even with regard to the apostles, except one (presumably John), "the disciple whom Jesus loved" (John 13:11). What are we to make of these statements? Jesus was supposed to be the example of perfect love. Perfect love is impartial. Why, then, did Jesus have special love for some people and not for others?

Perhaps the way to answer this question is to begin with the fact that friendship is not a moral problem. We become friends with some people, whereas others remain mere acquaintances. The reasons why some people become our friends run the gamut. At any rate, there is no inherent moral problem with the selectivity of friendship.

Thus, the idea that perfect love on the human plane requires an impartiality that rules out selectivity is untrue. We cannot show equal love (in the sense of being close to or intimate with) to all persons we meet. To relate closely takes time, attention, and energy. To relate equally to all would mean to relate superficially, as does a politician who shakes hands with a crowd.

We may say, then, that although Jesus revealed an impartial love by giving his life as a ransom for many (Mark 10:45), he simply could not be impartial in developing deep, close relationships. As a result, he selected for these special relationships "the disciple whom he loved," Mary, Martha, Lazarus, and others.

Now the question arises as to just what the essential nature of love is. The Greek philosopher Socrates held that love is desire, desire to possess its object. Socrates used the term "object" because he was thinking of ideals (such as beauty, justice, and truth) as well as persons. The Socratic concept of love emphasizes an aspect of love that still tends to dominate the thinking about love in our society: Love is rooted in the emotions, or love is essentially an emotion or feeling. To desire is not merely to have an antiseptic want but to have feelings for, to be attracted to, to have affection for, to care for, and so on. When we read that Jesus loved the rich young ruler, we are inclined to think of an immediate, spontaneous attraction to the young man. "Jesus looked at him and loved him" (Mark 10:17). Here was a man with whom Jesus could relate, a man with enthusiasm and earnestness for kingdom concerns. A spark flew from the man to Jesus, igniting Jesus' love. Ah, what a catch for the kingdom. What enthusiasm! What earnestness! What zeal! Yet . . . "My friend, I commend your enthusiasm for the things of God. You really need only one thing more in order to be a child of the kingdom."

"And what is that, Lord? I'm ready to do anything."

"All right, then go sell everything you have, give the proceeds to the poor, and come follow me."

Hesitation. The yoke of the kingdom or the yoke of mammon! O God, why must that be the choice? But the choice of the soul is the choice of priorities.   The young man went away sorrowfully. And so did Jesus. One who had so much potential, one who was so near to drinking from the fountain of life, went back to the stale waters of mammon.

Jesus was attracted to the rich young ruler and undoubtedly desired to possess him in the sense of having him as a disciple. "Come follow me," he had said. Thus, one form of love is desire, which is rooted in feelings and may be of varying degrees, from mild to very intense.

Love as desire often takes the form of what we call romantic love, love that invariably includes sexual attraction—whether outside of or within an established relationship of deep affection and care. The search for romantic love dominates the imagination of our society and has had a significant—and not an altogther happy—effect on our language. When sexual intercourse, even of the "one-night-stand" variety, is referred to as "making love," or when a child born out of wedlock to celebrities is referred to as a "child of love," then the word has truly been co-opted by culture. Our language clearly reveals the tendency to think of love in romantic terms, as a feeling or passion for another person. The feeling or passion may originate in a single encounter, as in *Romeo and Juliet*; thus the phrase "love at first sight." Naturally enough, the feeling may also vanish in a single encounter with another person; that is to say, we may have many loves at first sight. The point is that the feeling called love is volatile, disappearing now, reappearing later.

Jerry Lewis, for example, speaks of the end of his first marriage (a marriage of thirty-six years) in the following way: "There was no fun in my life. . . . I was bored, locked into routine. No fun." He remarks that he was indifferent to his wife; no feeling was left. Then, while casting for a movie, he met a dancer, had several dates with her, and "just like that, we were in love!"[1] Obviously, "just like that" he can be out of "love" again, as in the case of his first wife.

Jerry Lewis illustrates well the tendency to view love in romantic terms. No doubt love often does take the form of romantic feeling, which is certainly not inconsequential. Yet romantic love is a very limited form of love, mainly because it is so volatile. In short, romantic love is very frail and fickle, a truth painted with humorous brush by Cervantes in *Don Quixote*. In several passages Cervantes states the case against romantic love in so many words by way of his characters. For example, on the occasion of the wedding of Quiteria the fair to Camacho the rich, Cervantes has Don Quixote say:

> If all those who love one another were to marry . . . it would deprive parents of the right to choose, and marry their children to the proper person and at the proper time; and if it was left to daughters to choose husbands as they pleased, one would be for choosing her father's servant, and another, some one she has seen passing in the street and fancies gallant and dashing, though he may be a drunken bully; for love and fancy easily blind the eyes of the judgment, so much wanted in choosing one's way of life; and the matrimonial choice is very liable to error, and it needs great caution and the special favor of Heaven to make it a good one.[2]

Even Sancho Panza comes up with the following wisdom. Commenting on the devastation of Basilio the poor when he learned that his true love, Quiteria, was to marry Camacho, Sancho says:

> Between a woman's "yes" and "no" I wouldn't venture to put the point of a pin, for there would not be room for it; if you

tell me Quiteria loves Basilio heart and soul, then I'll give him a bag of good luck, for love, I have heard say, looks through spectacles that make copper seem gold, poverty, wealth; and blear eyes, pearls.[3]

We might add that the distance between a man's yes and no is certainly no greater than the distance between a woman's yes and no. We might also add that things worked out well for Basilio the poor, for by way of some bizarre happenings he, not Camacho, ended up marrying Quiteria.

Romantic love is fickle and as ephemeral as a rainbow. Of course, feelings in general are changeable. Even grief, we have seen, subsides. The person who thinks he will never get over his grief finds that as time passes, the sharpness of the grief dulls. So it is with romantic love; it can become dull or be totally lost. Actually, no feelings are more changeable than romantic love, although anger and hate are clearly just as volatile. We call all three of these feelings passions. They flame up as quickly as dry tinder but also die down as quickly as an unstoked fire. Those who think that they can construct an enduring, deepening relationship on a volatile passion alone are surely living in the world of make-believe. This conclusion is a general one, applying not merely to the relationship of marriage but also to friendship. Attraction alone is hardly a sufficient foundation for constructing a friendship. Feelings help and surely are not to be ignored in any friendship, but friendship also requires commitment, time, sharing, helping, and so on.

In addition to illustrating the tendency to view love in terms of romantic feeling, the marriages of Jerry Lewis illustrate our tendency to think of the feelings as outside our control. "They" just grab us, leaving us no choice but to go along with them. If we lose a feeling—as Lewis lost his feeling for his first wife—we just give up, assuming there is no way to regain the feeling. Yet feelings are not beyond our control.

Singh had been in graduate school for two years and in the United States for four years. Now he was about to get his degree and return to India; not to stay, for he was planning a career in the United States. He was going to India to "fetch a wife." Had she been his high school sweetheart? Not at all. Well, then, had they lived in the same neighborhood? No; in fact, he had seen her only a few times. So why was he marrying her? Because his family had made the arrangements with her family. If he positively detested her, he had veto power; however, his parents were prudent, reasonable people who had probably made a good choice. But how could he marry someone he didn't love? He could come to love her and care for her. His father had come to love his mother; his uncles, their wives; his friends, their wives. Why not him? What could be more natural than coming to love someone, than coming to have affection, feeling, for someone? Love is like a small seedling. You plant it, tend it, care for it, and it grows. Why not?

The fundamental problem with this scenario is that most people do not wish the discipline, indeed, the pain, of change and learning even though the resulting satisfaction would more than balance out the struggle. Jesus promised abundant life, but paradoxically (at least to us in the West, imbued as we are with ideas of hedonism) he also promised a narrow gate and a hard way. The path of the kingdom is admittedly a tough path because it is the path of continual change. Yet those who walk the path can testify that their life is anything but dull. Life on the path is an adventure, a highly satisfying adventure.

The multiple marriages of public figures illustrate the tendency to think that the dying of romantic love justifies breaking a relationship. If feelings have died and cannot be renewed, it is assumed that the only thing to do is to end the relationship.

Finally, multiple marriages illustrate the tendency to think that romantic love justifies just about anything with respect to a relationship. As long as we have feeling for ("care for") one another, marriages as well as extramarital affairs are justified. Our culture has come to view romantic love as the great "sanctifier" or "purifier" of relationships, no matter what the nature of the relationships.

Bill and Barbara were having difficulty with their marriages. In fact, Bill and his wife had been separated for a year. As for Barbara, she and her husband were struggling. She said that he had killed her feelings for him, that he lived in a different world, that he didn't understand her. Both Bill and Barbara had sung in the church choir for years. They had never paid much attention to each other, but somehow they began to talk more and more before choir, during breaks, and after choir. Gradually their common problems absorbed more and more of their conversations. They began having coffee together after choir rehearsal and sometimes after work. Barbara's husband was often out of town on business, so Bill and Barbara could easily see one another with no thought of discovery. The conversations became longer and longer until further time was required at Bill's house. Their activities seemed to raise not the slightest question in their minds. In choir they sang as lustily as ever, or perhaps more so! They listened attentively to the sermon, often discussing it afterward over coffee. Of course, Barbara's children had plenty of questions, as did Bill's, who were grown and out of the house. Yet for Bill and Barbara, the relationship was not problematic because they had "deep feelings" for one another. They even prayed together about their relationship. Their feelings, mixed with a pinch of prayer, sanctified everything, made everything perfect. Everything, however, was not perfect and Bill and Barbara eventually drifted back into their separate worlds of troubled marital relationships.

We are not saying that feeling is unimportant in relationships. Feeling, romantic feeling, is a highly important ingredient in a first-rate marriage. Similarly, romantic feeling outside of marriage (for example, in dating) is often anything but unimportant, trivial, or superficial. But romantic love, thought of strictly as a feeling for another person, is hardly a form of love on which we can pin hopes for a lasting, growing relationship or by which we can justify any kind of relationship we desire.

More importantly, romantic love is not the only, or the highest, form of love, a point apparent to anyone within Christianity. "God so loved the world" is the core of the gospel. But God's love is obviously not a romantic feeling. Even so, we would not begin to deny God's love or the high quality of his love, for God's love has been expressed in action, most notably in the giving of Jesus. "God was in Christ reconciling the world . . ." (2 Corinthians 5:19). Here we find God's love at the zenith of its expression in an act of giving and reconciling. Thus, from the Christian standpoint, love of the very highest form is essentially a certain kind of action.

"Love your neighbor as yourself" (Mark 12:31) is most decidedly a command with vast implications; yet whatever the full range of its implications, the command is instruction to act in a certain way. The good Samaritan did, indeed, feel; he felt compassion (Luke 10:33). As a matter of fact, compassion in the circumstances was appropriate and natural. However, Jesus commended the Samaritan not for his feeling of compassion but for *showing* mercy (Luke 10:36-37), that is, for *acting* neighborly or lovingly.

In the New Testament, then, neighbor-love is seen as involving action of a certain sort, namely, action in the best interests of another, action that aims to meet the needs of another. This minimum neighbor-love encompasses humankind's basic or minimum obligation to other human beings. It is action that neither requires that we know those who are the object of the action nor that we have feelings for them, although feelings of some sort—for example, sympathy, compassion, concern—are normally associated with the action.

Minimum neighbor-love is surely essential to life in the church. We are to relieve distress, provide for those in need, forgive, share God's gifts, and be patient with "one another in love, eager to maintain the unity of the Spirit in the bond of peace" (Ephesians 4:2-3). Further, we are to act in minimum neighbor-love as we reach out beyond the confines of the church in mission, clothing the unclothed, visiting the prisoners, comforting the crushed and bruised, seeking justice for the poor and oppressed, and proclaiming the good news of God's reconciling act in Christ.

Yet neighbor-love encompasses more than action in the best interests of another. It also encompasses what we might call "fellowship love," a love that reaches out to establish communion. Thus, just as God's love is a reaching out to us to establish communion and closeness, so must our love be. We must remember what was said earlier, namely, that various levels of communion exist. I may not be as close to a member of a small sharing group as I am to my wife or close friends, but I am closer to the person than I am to others outside the group because we have shared some of our important feelings with one another; we have learned of one another's needs, hurts, and joys; we have prayed together; we have wept together; we have laughed together.

Before concluding this section on love, let us focus on one more issue, the issue concerning love as affection. Some people do not seem very demonstrative about their affection for another. What shall we say about them? Does a person have to be demonstrative in order to be genuinely affectionate toward another? Or, more pointedly, why is there reluctance to demonstrate affection? One answer besides the conditioning of family or culture, is that a full expression of feeling makes us vulnerable—and we just do not want to be vulnerable. To break down and weep, for example, is to reveal ourselves unambiguously. If people know our feelings, they can hit us where we hurt. This same logic is often applied to issues of affection. To say, "I care very deeply for you" is to say, among other things, "I need you." But to say, "I need you" is to make oneself terribly vulnerable. It is, in effect, the erection of an emotional billboard. Yet in making ourselves vulnerable, we also make ourselves open to closeness. We demonstrate our essential humanity, saying, "I am not a piece of granite but a human who feels." In addition, by saying that we need another, we are laying the groundwork for loving relationships, for they are readily built on mutual need. Finally, we open ourselves by indicating that we are willing to share life with another. To say, "I need you" is to share life at a very significant level.

Even in the case of humor we are seeking to share and thus indicate our need of others. Who tells jokes to oneself? True, thinking about a good joke may bring a smile, but thinking about a joke does not begin to compare with sharing a joke with others. And what if people do not laugh at our jokes? In fact, what if they use our attempts at telling a joke to make fun of us? Yes, when we share humor, we also make ourselves vulnerable.

One caveat in conclusion is necessary. Although those who have committed themselves to the kingdom value of loving relationships accept the risk of vulnerability, they are not under any obligation to make themselves vulnerable to anybody, anywhere, anytime. The call to the kingdom is not a call to jettison prudence. If there are those who will take advantage of vulnerability, we have no reason to be vulnerable with those persons.

Joy

A positive emotion vital for our attention is joy. Joy signals the state of one's relationships.

In the writings of Paul joy is linked with love and peace. "The fruit of the spirit is love, joy, peace" (Galatians 5:21). "The kingdom of God is righteousness, peace, and joy in the Holy Spirit" (Romans 14:17). Since righteousness in the kingdom reduces essentially to loving relationships, we could read Romans 14:17 as, "The kingdom of God is love, peace, and joy in the Holy Spirit."

The linking of love and joy is hardly accidental. A life lived in pursuit of loving relationships is a life of satisfaction, of fulfillment. Joy is nothing less than the sense of satisfaction, a sense which may well up like a tidal surge or remain as a deep, calm pool. Joy signals success in living. Joy, we might say, is the Christian term for happiness. Joy is surely not identical with having fun, although anybody with good relationships is having fun—lots of it. Even in times of tragedy and serious sickness, those who are close will have plenty of laughs together, along with cries.

Since joy issues from success at relationships, it is more life-dependent than event-dependent; that is, it does not require some event in order to be felt or expressed. To be sure, Jesus expressed joy upon the successful mission of his disciples; however, what he rejoiced about was God's revelation to babes rather than to the worldly wise (Luke 10:21). Inasmuch as God's policy is constant, the cause for joy is constant. We can see from this example that joy issues not only from success at relationships but also from a deep appreciation for and satisfaction in the person, policies, and actions of God, particularly the actions of God in Christ. We delight in, we joy in, all that God has done, is doing, and will do in Christ. Joy is the result of a lifestyle modeled after Christ, a lifestyle focused on God and others. To fail to pursue the lifestyle is to fail to have joy.

Leo Tolstoy's story "The Death of Ivan Ilyich" is most instructive.[4] Ivan was an immensely self-centered man, caring only for his own pleasure, power, status, comfort, and wealth. His wife and children were simply necessary baggage; a man of his standing was expected to have a family. But he cared little for them; in fact, Ivan positively disliked being around his wife. She was too demanding, too insistent that he give her his time and devotion. Then

Ivan fell sick and began to taste what he had dished out. His family saw him as a burden, not as a loving father who was slipping away day by day. The only person who expressed genuine concern for him was his simple peasant servant, Gerizim. Ivan was alone in the world, except for Gerizim. Finally, after much physical suffering and mental anguish, Ivan realized the utter disaster of his life, a life lived without love, without caring, without close relationships. His last act, however, was an act of love—he asked for forgiveness, though his family did not understand his words, and then relinquished his hold on life, thus releasing his family from further suffering. The result was joy.

Conclusion

In the last two chapters we have seen Jesus expressing a range of feelings and emotions. In doing so, he clearly demonstrated his humanity, as do we when we express feelings and emotions. In declaring our humanity, we declare ourselves to be relating beings. Moreover, in expressing our feelings, we show ourselves willing to share even at the risk of being hurt. By showing ourselves willing to share, we open ourselves to others, enabling our search for loving relationships that share not only the peripheral but the core concerns of our lives. By expressing our feelings, we declare ourselves willing to share life at its deepest levels.

Observing the range of emotions Jesus expressed, from the tender emotion of sympathy to the strong emotion of anger, we note that emotions do not easily divide along a gender line. The idea that certain emotions, or the expression of them, are male whereas others are female is one of the many myths of Western culture. A male can be as tender and sensitive as any female and a female can be as aggressive and violent as any male.

Trying to ascribe some emotions to males and others to females may be symptomatic of the pervasive disease of self-deception. In any case, self-deception is one of the central problems with respect to the affective life. Far too often we say or believe what we are expected to say or believe. If as God's children we are supposed to have joy, then we put on our "Smile, Jesus loves you!" masks, regardless of how grim we might feel. Several psychological studies indicate a tendency for Christians to rate themselves to be more in line with Christian values than psychological tests rate them.[5] Informal observation supports these studies. Thus, we have the strong suspicion that self-deception is endemic to the church.

A fundamental reason why self-deception is endemic to the church is that it is endemic to our culture, as it has been to cultures from time immemorial. For example, we often wax eloquent about the glories of fifth-century Athens, yet everything about fifth-century Athens was not glorious, especially the Athens of the latter fifth century, the Athens which executed Socrates (399 B.C.) on the trumped-up charges of impiety and corrupting the youth.

The religious establishment in Jesus' day was no different. Those in the seat of authority could not endure the light of one who demanded the jettisoning of sham, pretense, and superficiality in religion. Therefore, they—the ones cloaked in sham, pretense, and superficiality—accused Jesus of being a threat to the religion of the patriarchs and to the peace and stability of the nation (John 11:45-50). As in the case of Socrates, the leaders eliminated this upstart "prophet" who had the audacity to unmask their self-deception.

Self-deception, then, is anything but new; and it remains very much alive and well in our culture. Recently I listened to an offensive guard on a professional football team state that offensive linemen engage in holding 90 percent of the time when pass-blocking. Without this help, he said, the quarterback would be sacked continually, the game would become dull, and fans would not turn out. He was good at rationalizations. He was also good at illegal blocking.

He had "succeeded" not in reforming but in hiding his violations so well that he hardly ever got caught. Perhaps this was one reason why he was a starter!

Further examples of self-deception crowd into our mind: rationalizing the use of drugs (steroids, amphetamines) in sports; rationalizing fudging on income tax forms; rationalizing overindulgence; rationalizing political demagoguery, half-truths, and propaganda; rationalizing the projection of an image that has little to do with reality; rationalizing membership in groups that unjustly exclude people on the basis of race, religion, or sex; rationalizing inadequate programs for the poor and weak; rationalizing the use of violence in response to violence—the list could go on indefinitely.

Of course, if we simply let ourselves reflect, all our rationalizations are absurd. The words of Jesus come piercing through the fog of self-deception: "Let your yes be yes and your no, no" (Matthew 5:37); "Unless your righteousness exceeds that of the scribes and Pharisees, you will never enter the kingdom of heaven" (Matthew 5:20). Jesus' words remind us that self-honesty is essential for personal growth and for developing loving relationships.

In addition, our relationship with God will go nowhere as long as we are anything but honest with ourselves. If we are angry with God, we must face the anger. If we feel distant from God, we need to shout with Jesus and the psalmist, "My God, my God, why have you forsaken me?" There is little use in trying to deceive God, before whom our inner thoughts play like a videotape (Psalm 139:1-4).

The real issue of the affective life is ultimately the issue of what Jesus calls us to be. He calls us to be people who are caring, people who can get close to other people, people who have relationships that are deep and enduring. In order to be such people we shall need to be people who feel and express feeling appropriately, under the rule of our reason and moral judgment. Jesus himself has provided a human and healthy sketch of having and express-

ing emotions that are conducive to the best in human relationships. The details of that sketch remain to be filled
in by his followers.

5

Jesus and Individual Attention

Nathan had been looking forward to his first year in college. High school had been a "blast," but he was more than ready to move on. In fact, he had already chosen his career; he was going to be a psychiatrist. Already he knew more about the major figures in psychology than any of his teachers. He had found his senior year subjects relatively easy, so he had time to devour every book on psychology that he could find. Now September was here, and he was off to the university.

The first day of class was a bit of a shock. In particular, he couldn't believe the size of two of his classes. His chemistry class and his history class were held in auditoriums, with about 400 students in one, more than 500 in the other. The chemistry professor turned out to be a brilliant teacher, something of an actor, with new stunts every day. Obviously the professor didn't have the faintest idea who Nathan was or any of the other students. All grading of exams and answering of questions were taken care of in the lab sections, which were run by graduate assistants. Getting in to see the professor was simply impossible. The man was engaged in high-level research and couldn't be bothered with elementary freshman questions.

Realizing that he simply had to have chemistry, Nathan settled down and adjusted to the system as well as he could. He figured that things would get better as he progressed into higher level courses.

Nathan had real trouble, though, adjusting to his history course. There was the same chasm between professor and students but there were no lab sections, only graders. Moreover, the professor was a renowned scholar, but boring! Why not stick him in the archives rather than in front of freshman students? Nathan was disgusted. In high school he had loved history. Even old coach Buford had managed to keep Nathan's interest in ancient history. But this fellow was something else. He had, amidst his other faults, a most distracting habit. He was a chain smoker who never took his cigarette out of his mouth. As he droned on, the cigarette bounced up and down in his mouth, distracting Nathan along with most of the rest of the class. To top things off, Nathan's tests got mixed up with another student's, whose name was similar. Nathan went to the grader but was intercepted by a secretary who sent him to another grader—the wrong one. Nathan didn't get the names straightened out until after mid-semester, and the same mix-up occurred again on the final examination. Nathan realized he was caught in a vast impersonal web. He was just a name on a roll, followed by a social security number, followed by courses and grades, all of which were hidden in a huge computer. Nathan was not pleased.

Nor can anyone else be pleased with being treated simply as a number or a product. (The corporate model has become popular among many school administrators. In the model, students are viewed as products of the corporation, the university.) Yet we live in a society which engages in the mass processing of people, just as it engages in the mass production of goods. The mass approach is seen as necessary because it is cost effective even though it may be, at the same time, destructive of persons. If cost-effectiveness takes precedence over recognizing and treating another as a person, then we are in a system in full conflict with kingdom values. Unfortunately, that is exactly the sort of a system in which we are, with few exceptions. Moreover, the system is aggravated by advertising designed to manipulate more than inform, mass advertising often not remotely connected with truth or reality.

Edgar had banked for years with the Old Main bank. He had a personal loan officer, one of his friends in the church. When he had a cash flow problem in his shoe repair business, he would go to Bob and within the hour have the needed cash. If Edgar was getting too far in debt, Bob would let him know, sitting down with him to see what could be done to improve cash flow or to get the loan payments reduced.

Last year Old Main was bought out by a holding company that began an aggressive billboard and TV advertising campaign. "Old Main is personalized banking," ran the ads; "We are a people bank"; and so on. The problem for Edgar was that Bob had been encouraged to leave. New officers from the central office had been brought in and given the status, privileged positions. Months passed before Edgar was assigned a new loan officer, and then the officer had virtually no power—at least as far as Edgar could tell. "The credit committee has a probelm with your collateral," he heard; "the other officers on the committee want more information about your loan at Central Bank"; "the committee meets only once a week, so I can't give you an answer until next Tuesday"; and so it went. This was not personalized banking in Edgar's mind. Yet the advertising campaign continued.

We live in a society of media blitz, of mass appeal. Either advertisers work up profiles of the typical consumer, aiming their appeal at this artificial creature, or they try to create a mass "need" for a product, through manipulation.

Even in the religious sphere there is mass, impersonal appeal, most evident in the computerized electronic church. Everybody gets the same "personal" letter from the TV evangelist. Everybody must follow the same routine for getting saved or healed. Everybody must follow the chosen method for winning souls. Everything is packaged and smooth. There are three *easy* steps to salvation, two *easy* steps to soul-winning, and one *easy* step to sending in your money.

It is no wonder that people turn to the Unification Church or to Hare Krishna, because these groups have learned to zero in—at least during the proselytizing period—on peoples' needs for friendship, attention, acceptance, and concern. Many people will turn to just about any group as long as it promises them that they will be somebody. Unfortunately, the promises of many groups, particularly the cult-type groups, usually far exceed what is finally delivered. Once the "Moonies" get their disciple, the disciple becomes just another drone or worker bee. Similarly, the Hare Krishna disciples become reproductions of one another, dressing alike, cutting their hair alike, eating alike, speaking alike, and so on.

Things are no better in the drug cults. In reading about the psychedelic sessions of Timothy Leary (particularly after he left Harvard), one observes that the drugs, which were supposed to be consciousness expanding and which were supposed to demolish barriers between persons, did nothing of the sort, except in a few instances.[1] The drugs became crutches to personal pleasure. Instead of enlarging consciousness to focus on others in their full individuality, the drugs served simply to enhance concentration on the world of one's particular experience. Others really became irrelevant. There is no greater depersonalization than that!

The Call of the Apostles

We have noted that a slice of religion today is electronic and computerized, geared for mass appeal. The call to faith is often a mass call: "Bow your head and repeat after me this prayer of repentance. Then send us your name and we will send you material that will aid you in beginning your Christian life."

There is no reason to urge the cancellation of mass appeals and approaches. Radio, television, the mass crusade, can all play a role in disseminating the gospel. People have been genuinely converted by mass or packaged appeals that do not suit me or do not strike me as especially appropriate or even biblical. I have long been critical of what we might call hitchhiker evangelism in which a driver picks up hitchhikers and gives them the packaged pitch for Jesus. Yet I also recall an acquaintance, a child of the sixties, solidly into drugs, who was converted because of a witness in a car. He was hitchhiking home from a drug scene in the northeast when he was picked up and told about Christ. When he got out of the car, he immediately prayed a prayer, which not even he can fully remember, and began his Christian life, a life that has been sustained now for many years.

Although mass, packaged evangelism plays a role in disseminating the gospel, the mass approach has hardly proved to be the most consistently effective. I remember following up with other church members seventy people who had declared themselves for Christ during a Billy Graham crusade. Only one of the seventy showed even a slight interest in pursuing the decision further, particularly in the way of getting active in a local church. When asked what "going forward" meant to them, most said: "It made me feel better." This is a pleasant enough result but not even remotely related to the call to Christian discipleship. Yet I know several people who were thoroughly converted in a Graham crusade and since their conversion have exercised considerable influence for Christ in the church or in Christian social action projects.

Perhaps the point to make is this: We cannot write off the mass media and thus the mass approach to evangelism, but we also dare not limit ourselves to the mass approach. Even a quality mass approach to calling people to the kingdom will hit some but miss many others. I am able to wear mass-produced suits, but a number of my friends could not wear a suit bought off a rack if their lives depended on it. More importantly, the value changes expected of us as children of the kingdom necessitate zeroing in on specific deficiencies, as well as expressing and receiving forgiveness, affirmation, and acceptance. These are requirements that can be met only by personal, individual contact.

When Jesus called to discipleship those who later became his apostles, he did so on an individual basis, singling them out personally. He gave no mass invitation. Instead, he went where they were, to their places of work, giving them a direct, person-to-person call.

James, John, Peter, and Andrew were mending their nets beside the Sea of Galilee. They had undoubtedly heard Jesus teach and seen him heal; they had been with the crowds, perhaps staying around after most others left in order to ask Jesus further questions. Peter and Andrew had had personal contact with Jesus some weeks earlier when they had traveled to Judaea to see and hear John the Baptist (John 1:35-42). Now Jesus was looking for more than interest in his teaching and healing. Jesus did not want spectators, but followers who would go long-term for the kingdom. He was after disciples. Therefore, he called them individually, avoiding any of the techniques of crowd psychology. The person who knows even the slighest bit about crowd psychology can get people in a crowd to shout, clap hands, come forward, or do violence to members of some other group. Yet Jesus was not interested in the techniques of mass persuasion; he was not after a signature on the line which would either be regretted the next day or at least not followed up with action. He was after people who would go with him through the valley of the shadow of death. Thus, he employed no gimmicks. He used no crowd pressure. He went to these men where they were working and said simply, ''Follow me.''

Jesus also called Matthew personally at the tax office where Matthew worked (Matthew 9:9). Philip was another to whom Jesus went personally ("Jesus found Philip," John 1:43). We do not know exactly how Jesus first called the rest of the apostles to discipleship, but we do know that when he selected twelve to be apostles, he selected them from a broader group of disciples (Luke 6:12-13); *he* selected them personally, one by one.

The fact that Jesus chose twelve to be close to him is perhaps the clearest evidence of the personal, individualized nature of Jesus' ministry. Although Jesus ministered to the masses and to a broader group of disciples, he concentrated on the apostles. He taught them in depth; he stayed with them constantly; he sent them on preaching and teaching missions; he prayed with them; he rebuked and corrected them; he accepted and forgave them, regardless of how narrow or dull they were. Even among the twelve, he selected three—Peter, James, and John—to receive a greater portion of his personal attention. They were the only apostles permitted to witness the healing of Jairus's daughter (Mark 5:37) and the transfiguration (Mark 9:2); further, they were selected to be closest to Jesus in the Garden of Gethsemene in his hour of need (Mark 14:33-35).

Jesus and Peter

Although Jesus' concentration on the twelve is probably the clearest evidence of the personal nature of his ministry, his treatment of Peter is especially significant, demonstrating with great poignancy the sensitivity of Jesus to the individual.

The miracle of the fish (Luke 5:1-11) seems designed just for Peter, the big, blustering fisherman. Peter has seen Jesus heal and listened to him teach and is duly impressed, although far from being able to fathom who Jesus really is. One morning Jesus uses Peter's boat to teach the crowds. After dismissing the crowds he turns to Peter and tells him to shove off into deep water and let down his nets. Peter is anything but thrilled with Jesus' command. "Jesus, the fish just aren't around today. We fished all night and came up with nothing but some junk fish. What do you think we'll catch now? But . . . if you say so. . . ."

Off Peter went into deep water with Andrew, his brother. When they put down their nets, they hit such a school of fish that they had to call for their partners, James and John, to come and help. Where did this school of fish come from? How did Jesus know it was here? Peter had only one answer to these questions. After reaching shore with his boat half under water, the fish spilling over the side, he jumped out and threw himself at Jesus' feet, exclaiming, "Depart from me, for I am a sinful man, O Lord!"

This incident was undoubtedly crucial to Peter's conception of Jesus. Later, when Jesus asked his disciples who he was (Matthew 16:13-27), Peter jumped forward before the others could even think, saying, "You are the Christ, the Son of the living God." Upon hearing this confession, Jesus directed a personal commendation to Peter: "Blessed are you, Peter, for you have been listening carefully to the voice of God" (vv. 17-18). Then Jesus went on to promise Peter a dominant role in the church.

Yet Peter had really listened only selectively to God's voice, for when Jesus continued by saying that he was soon to be put to death, Peter brashly told Jesus he was mistaken. There was no way the Christ, the Messiah, would be rejected and put to death—either by Jews or Romans! Jesus' response was immediate and withering, directed specifically at Peter, "Out of my sight, Peter, for you are speaking and acting as Satan; you are speaking and acting in opposition to the will of God" (Matthew 16:23).

Jesus had not given up on Peter, though. In his very next breath he reached out to Peter, inviting him to discipleship, making clear, however, the conditions of discipleship. "If any one wants to come after me, he must deny himself, take up his cross daily, and follow me." "Peter," Jesus was saying, "not only am I going to suffer and die, but I'm calling you to the same. You simply have to understand that I am the Servant of the Lord, and the Servant of the Lord suffers and dies for his people, as my disciple, you too are called to the role of suffering servant, called to suffer, even to die, for the kingdom" (see Matthew 16:24-27; Isaiah 53).

Peter definitely did not understand all that Jesus said, but he did understand that all was on the line, and he was not about to leave Jesus. If he must take up a cross, then he would take up a cross.

Unhappily, Peter completely flunked his first real test in cross bearing. The night before the crucifixion Jesus predicted that the apostles would abandon him in the hours of his final battle. That was just too much for Peter. "Jesus," Peter had responded, "you may not be able to depend on these other fellows but, Lord, it's always at least you and me!" (see Luke 22:33). Jesus replied by detailing exactly how Peter would abandon Jesus. Peter, however, would have nothing of Jesus' warning; neither would the other apostles.

Approaching the hour of his most decisive battle with the hosts of evil, Jesus went to pray in the Garden, singling out Peter, James, and John to be especially close to him. Yet in his hour of need and their hour of need they fell asleep. Jesus, returning to them after anguishing in prayer, zeroed in on Peter. "Come now, Peter, are you asleep? Couldn't you stay awake just one hour? Tell me, Peter, what if you had been on watch in the Roman army and I had been your commander? What do you think would have happened? Yet you tell me that you will stick with me to the end. Peter, you are far too cocky. You need not fall, but I assure you that as long as you will not recognize your own weakness, you will definitely fall" (see Mark 14:37-38). Unfortunately, the message sailed right over Peter's head with the result that Peter fulfilled Jesus' prediction in detail.

But Jesus was still not through with Peter. On the day of resurrection he appeared to Peter before any of the other apostles (1 Corinthians 15:3-5). We do not know what Peter said or did or what Jesus said or did on the occasion, but the occasion was surely one of confession and forgiveness for Peter. Even so, Peter easily could have thought that he was washed up as a leader in the church. After failing Jesus so miserably, how could he possibly exercise leadership? He had lost all credibility. True, the other apostles had not done much better than he; yet they had not explicitly denied Jesus. True, Jesus had forgiven. However, forgiveness was one thing; leadership in the church was quite another.

Peter desperately needed to be reassured of his central role in the church and he needed to be reassured in the presence of the other apostles. Thus Jesus appeared to the apostles at the Sea of Galilee. After breakfasting with them, he turned to Peter and said, "Peter, do you love me more than these?" The exact meaning of Jesus' question is not clear. Did he mean, "Do you love me more than the other apostles love me?" or "Do you love me more than you love your fellow apostles?" or "Do you love me more than these things, all that is associated with the old life—the crisp morning air, the slapping of the waves against the boat, the struggle with the nets, the comradery of those who have fought the winds on the sea?" Whatever Jesus' exact meaning, he was clearly asking about Peter's love. To Peter's credit, he focused on that issue. "Yes, Lord," he answered, "you know that I love you." What else was there to say? Peter had failed Jesus; Jesus knew that. Peter had anguished over his failure; Jesus knew that, too. Moreover, Peter had anguished over his failure basically because he loved Jesus. So what else was there to say but, "Yes, Jesus, you know that I love you." "Then feed my lambs, Peter." Unambiguously, Jesus affirmed Peter's role of caring for the weak, the young. Peter was weak; though through his weakness he had become stronger. Now he would be more sensitive to the lambs, to the weak, to the young in the faith. When the lambs fell into a crevice or went astray, Peter, rather than raging and blustering, would react with sensitivity and tenderness, remembering that he, too, had gone astray. "Peter, feed my lambs," said Jesus.

Still, Jesus repeated his question: "Peter, do you love me?" Jesus knew the impulsiveness of Peter. He wanted Peter to think the question through carefully. Thus, he asked Peter about his love three times (see John 21:15-17).

Having affirmed Peter as a keeper of the flock after having said, in effect, "Peter, you are ready now to take care of my sheep," Jesus went on to affirm Peter further by telling him he would suffer and die for Jesus' sake. Jesus was saying: "Peter, you were so weak that you denied me before a little servant girl and a sarcastic group of bystanders. Now you are a stronger man; yes, and you will become even stronger. You will become strong enough to suffer and die for me. I assure you that your original promise to me, to go with me to death, will be fulfilled. You may have dishonored me at one time, but now you will honor me greatly" (see John 21:18-19). Affirmation! Peter needed it. Jesus gave it to him in abundance.

What we discover from Jesus' treatment of Peter is that the individualizing route merges with the route leading to affirmation, acceptance, and forgiveness. To approach people in their full individuality is to recognize and accept them for who they are, not as abstractions, faces in a crowd, numbers on a computer card.

How often we hear entertainers, not to mention the clergy, exclaim to a crowd, "I love you all!" Loving in the abstract is uncomplicated, tidy, and easy. Abstract love experiences none of the messy idiosyncracies and irritating habits of people; none of the denials and betrayals; none of the unfaithfulness and inconsistencies; none of the contrariness and obstinacy; none of the broken promises and abandonments; in short, none of the reality of living, breathing human beings. Easy love—how nice. Perhaps it is not really so nice after all, for unless we wade out of the shallows of abstraction into the deep waters of real individuality, we shall know nothing of the satisfactions of closeness and communion. Taking the individual approach to loving relationships is a matter of placing ourselves on a path requiring affirmation and acceptance of persons in their concrete reality. The path may be longer, but it leads to abundant living.

Brad just couldn't believe it. The parents of one of his university English students were coming to see him because their daughter was getting C's on her essays. Unbelievable! One reason Brad had labored to get his Ph.D was to get away from what he called the "Mickey Mouse stuff" in high school teaching. Now he was right back into it. He thought he was working with adults, but some parents didn't view their children in college as adults.

They were complaining with their first breath. "Debby made B's and A's in high school, mostly A's. What's the explanation for the C's?"

"Actually, a C is not a bad grade for a freshman student," he had responded. "In fact, Debby is about the best in her class."

"The best in her class? Then why isn't she getting A's?"

"Because I don't grade on the class average," Brad said. "I grade according to university-level writing standards."

The conversation went nowhere. Brad saw immediately that Debby's parents wanted a daughter who was an A student. She was okay, would get strokes, would be affirmed as long as she got high grades. There was no thought of accepting and affirming her for what she was in her individuality, a girl with average scholastic aptitude. What was really sad in Brad's mind was that the parents were more concerned about their image. They wanted Debby to make them look good.

Brad had come across this type of parent time and time again. He remembered Bud, who, with tears in his eyes, told Brad how he wanted to be an artist. In his art courses he made straight A's and, more importantly, he loved the courses. However, his father would have none of "this effeminate art business." His son was going to be an engineer. Yet Bud hated engineering and was about to be dropped out of the program because of poor grades, even though he was bright enough to handle the courses and even though his father had threatened to cut off Bud's support unless he "got his act together." Bud's father had also told him that not one thin dime would ever come his way for an art course. Bud's father was not at all accepting of his son's individuality!

The call of Jesus is to accept and affirm individuals. It is also to accept and affirm those who fail in the true sense of failure. Jesus affirmed the one who betrayed him. How much more, then, are we called to accept and affirm those who fail to meet our arbitrarily imposed expectations? Indeed, what we are really called to do is to reform our expectations.

Jesus and Judas

The Gospels tell us very little about Judas. He was apparently the treasurer for the apostles (John 12:6) and not a very honest one at that. The fact that he was treasurer indicates that Jesus singled him out for a position of special trust and responsibility, thereby extending to him Jesus' acceptance and love.

Jesus also singled out Judas for rebuke on the occasion of the supper at Bethany (John 12:1-8; Mark 14:3-9). Mary poured ointment on the feet of Jesus, an act which called forth biting criticism from Judas. "Why wasn't the money used to purchase this ointment given to the poor?" he asked.

"Leave her alone," said Jesus. "You will always have the poor around. You will never lack occasion to do them good; but you will not always have me around. Mary realizes this, and so she has done a very beautiful, loving thing."

There was rebuke for Judas; strokes for Mary, who apparently was far ahead of the apostles in grasping Jesus' words about his death. Even in commending Mary, Jesus was also asking Judas, "How about your love? What has happened to it? What can be more important than loving? Even if you reject me as the promised one of Israel, do you have to seek my harm?" Jesus' rebuke was also a call for Judas to turn from his dark intentions; it was an expression of Jesus' forgiveness and acceptance.

Perhaps the event which most clearly reveals Jesus' personal attention to Judas is the Last Supper, the supper on the evening when Judas betrayed Jesus (John 13:21-30). Judas was reclining close to Jesus, so close that Jesus could whisper to him or hand him a morsel from the table. At that time the custom when eating was to recline on pillows around a low table, lying on the left elbow with the right hand free to take food and drink from the table. The beloved disciple was reclining immediately in front of Jesus, close to Jesus' breast. Judas was apparently just behind Jesus, in the position which was second only to that of Jesus, a point which surely cannot have been lost on Judas. When Jesus said that one of the twelve would betray him, the twelve instantly reacted, each one asking, "Is it I, Master?" Judas' question was, however, a whispered, "Is it I, rabbi?" The whispered reply was, "You have said so" (Matthew 26:20-25). So Jesus had found him out. Did any of the others know? What would they do if they found out? While these questions raced through the mind of Judas, Peter beckoned to John to find out who the betrayer was. John, lying close to Jesus, whispered his query. Jesus quietly said that the traitor was the one to whom he would give the unleavened bread after he dipped it in the common dish. He then dipped the bread and handed it to Judas—an act, by custom, of friendship (see John 13:26). Jesus was making one last effort to declare his love for

Judas, to offer him forgiveness and acceptance, to rescue him from the abyss. Yet this very personal and loving act of Jesus only triggered Judas' hostility, his resolve to eliminate Jesus. Judas jumped up from the table and went out into the night.

Crystal had become addicted to PCPs ("angel dust") and had drifted from one place to another. She became pregnant, had an abortion, and finally ended up in jail. Her parents had not heard from her for months, even though they had tried desperately to locate her. They anguished over their daughter and over themselves. How had they failed? Bob and Gail had been very accepting, listening, sensitive parents. They had had little trouble with their two younger children, but Crystal. . . . What happened? The question would just not go away.

At two in the morning a call came from the police station in a distant city. The voice . . . the weeping voice was Crystal's. Praise God! Crystal has been found! "Daddy, they have me on a prostitution charge. . . ."

"Honey . . . Crystal! Look, you just sit tight. Mom and I will be there tomorrow afternoon. We'll bail you out, and . . . do you want to come home with us?"

"Oh, Daddy . . . do you really mean it?"

"Do I mean it? Honey, I've never meant anything more!"

So a tortuous saga of rehabilitation began. Crystal was in bad shape, having used drugs consistently. Bob and Gail placed her in a rehabilitation center for several months. They chose the center because of its reputation for personalized care, practically going bankrupt to do so. After Crystal's system cleared of drugs, her parents took her home. They tried not to hover over her but to express trust and confidence in her, being sensitive and responsive to where she was at each step of her rehabilitation. Within six months she was able to take part-time employment.

She seemed to be returning to society, attending church and participating in youth functions, as well as going to various community events. After a year she started college, with plans to pursue a degree in psychological counseling. And then suddenly, unexpectedly, like a bursting bubble, she was gone. Gone!

Bob and Gail were crushed. For over a year they literally had poured their lives into Crystal, even to the neglect of their younger son and daughter. And with what result? They frantically tried to find Crystal. They heard she was with an aunt in the West. Bob flew out immediately—only to find that Crystal had disappeared. After four years she is still missing, perhaps not even alive. If she is ever found, Bob and Gail will go through everything again . . . and again. Even though Crystal betrayed their acceptance and trust, they will not give up on her—ever.

Jesus and the Paralytic

Early in his ministry (Mark 2:1-12), Jesus returned to Capernaum after a mission of teaching and healing in the surrounding cities. Immediately the news was out; Jesus was back. Women finished kneading their dough, old men stopped their conversations, children interrupted their playing, and even workmen laid down their tools in order to go to the teacher's home. Soon a crowd had gathered, calling for Jesus, asking him to tell them more about God's kingdom. Although Jesus was exhausted, he appeared in the doorway, greeted the crowd warmly, and began to teach the people, responding to the many questions they had. "What do you mean, the kingdom of God is near?" "Will Gentiles enter the kingdom?" "Why will the Pharisees have such trouble entering the kingdom, more trouble than tax collectors and harlots?" "How can a person be pure in heart?"

As he responded to the questions, often illustrating his points with parables, four men came carrying a young paralytic man on a litter. They tried to make their way through the crowd, but the crowd was not interested in making a way for the men. "Relax, you can get to Jesus later," said a man in the crowd. "Keep it down. He's right in the middle of a story," said another. "Quit pushing. I'm hardly able to breathe now." "What's the rush? Jesus isn't going to run away, you know."

The men were single-minded, though. They were going to get to Jesus and get to him now. They went around to the side of the house where a staircase led up to the roof. Once on the roof, they quickly tore open a hole in the roof large enough to get the litter through. Several in the front of the crowd started whispering and pointing to the inside of the house. Jesus turned to see the hole in the roof, with the men peering down. He quickly called several men out of the crowd to assist in lowering the litter to the floor of the house.

When the paralytic was placed on the floor, Jesus, without waiting for him to speak, said, "Son, your sins are forgiven." There was not a word said about healing. Just, "Son, your sins are forgiven." Jesus did not normally proceed in this way. What was on his mind?

Jesus undoubtedly sensed a special need, a need for forgiveness and affirmation. He was well aware of the connection in the popular mind between sickness, suffering, and sin. People insisted on linking implicitly, if not explicitly, sin and sickness: If a person had some sort of sickness or disease, chances were that he or she had abused God's law. No doubt the paralytic had been bombarded with the sin-sickness theology for so long that he had begun to believe it. He had begun to lose his sense of self-worth, often sliding into periods of acute depression. His friends saw that something had to be done immediately. Hearing that Jesus had returned to town, they brought their friend to Jesus as soon as they could.

Jesus, in forgiving the man, was by no means endorsing the views of his contemporaries about sin and sickness. He was simply focusing on the most fundamental need of the man, the need the paralytic felt most, the need for forgiveness. Altough the paralytic was wrong in thinking that his paralysis was linked to his sin, he was definitely not wrong in thinking of himself as a sinner, as one who had fallen short of God's law, as one who needed forgiveness. Thus, the paralytic needed a word from God, a word of forgiveness. When Jesus spoke that word, a look of immense relief and then joy came over the face of the paralytic. "I'm forgiven, forgiven!" he must have thought. "Why, I feel almost as if I had been untied, unbound. God be praised!"

Of course, Jesus had not finished with the young man, who would receive from Jesus not only the spiritual freedom of forgiveness but also the bodily freedom of the full use of his limbs. Jesus looked at the young man and said, "Rise, take up your pallet and walk," a command which was not just a demonstration of Jesus' power over disease but also a call to the young man to participate in the healing process and to reenter society. Jesus was, in effect, saying: "You have been totally dependent on others for years. Now that is all ended. You are not to forget how much you need others; but you are to return to a way of life in which you bear your own share of the load." Unquestionably, the young man needed to hear this personal word to him.

As for Jerry, he had gone into a shell. He would stay in his room all day, staring at the walls, listening to rock music, and chain-smoking. His parents had hoped that he would go on to college and pursue a communications degree, as he had planned; but for some reason Jerry had withdrawn into himself. He actually feared coming out of his room, not to mention his house. Jerry was a social paralytic.

His parents tried everything they could think of to motivate a change in his behavior. They tried sending him to several psychiatrists, with little success. Jerry would seem to improve for a brief time and then revert to his original behavior. Finally Jerry's parents found a counselor who agreed to work with Jerry as long as he could work with them, too. Jerry's parents didn't know why they needed counseling, but they were willing to do anything they could to get Jerry back to normality.

Jerry was a reluctant patient. Yet if his parents would go, yes, he'd go. That was about all he did at the beginning. He sat close-mouthed and unresponsive. After weeks of seemingly getting nowhere, the counseling sessions began to move. Jerry perked up, listening carefully to every word. Then he began to make brief comments. Slowly he began to open up. He ventured out of his room into the backyard. He called an old friend. The progress was slow but constant. Today he has been working for two months in a local hospital and has been dating a girl he met there. He is not totally "out of the woods" but is on his way because of a counselor who tailored his methods to Jerry's needs and because of parents who carried him with patience, persistence, faith, and acceptance through the healing process.

Jesus and the Rich Young Ruler

When the rich young nobleman ran up to Jesus, kneeling before him, asking him about eternal life, Jesus instantly seemed to feel a warmth for the young man (Mark 10:17-

21). "Jesus looking upon him loved him" (v. 21). Surely the young man could not miss that special look of Jesus, a special look of love specifically directed at the young man. Just as surely the young man could not miss the special call of Jesus: "Go, sell what you have, and give to the poor . . . and come, follow me" (v. 21).

The call was, indeed, special. Jesus did not ask the apostles to give up all they had before they came after him. Peter, Andrew, James, and John neither sold their boats nor their homes. Jesus may well have owned his home. The issue here seems to be attachment to possessions, not simply having possessions. One may have great possessions and yet be detached from them; that is, they could all be removed in a day without any loss of peace, tranquility, or joy.

The problem with the rich young man was that he was attached to and fettered by his possessions. Jesus zeroed in on the young man's problem. "Go sell all that you have." The young man was like the alcoholic who needed to make a clean break with anything even faintly resembling alcohol. The young man would never get possessions out of his system except by selling them all. To be bound to the kingdom, he must be unbound from things. Thus came the words, "Go sell what you have." And then Jesus added: "Give to the poor, and come, follow me." Jesus was unambiguously underscoring the fact that the life of the kingdom is a servant life, a life of ministering to the poor, the weak, the oppressed, a life that will never be pursued seriously by anyone attached to things. Persons, not things, are important in the kingdom.

"Young man," Jesus was saying, "you say you have kept the commandments. You say you love God with all your heart, soul, and might. But to love God with all the soul is to love the purposes of God: those purposes focus on persons. Your purposes, young man, focus on your wealth and you are a divided, unhappy man. You know that you are lacking even with the sufficiency of your wealth. Otherwise, why did you come running to me inquiring about eternal life, inquiring about the means to fill that emptiness in your soul? I am telling you how to fill that emptiness, how to obtain the life of true abundance. Go sell all that you have, give the proceeds to the poor, and come follow me."

Sadly, the young man walked away. The grip of his wealth was too strong to be broken either by a loving gaze or by a personalized formula for achieving abundant life.

In our modern world of mass communications the personalized formula tends to get replaced by the generalized, impersonal formula. Unfortunately, the generalized, impersonal formula does not work in the case of Christian discipleship. The television evangelist repeats the formula, "Believe in the Lord Jesus Christ," a formula that is thoroughly biblical. Yet believing in the Lord Jesus Christ means, among other things, taking on the lordship of Christ, a lordship that has immediate implications for the individual. If I am the publisher of a pornographic magazine, then I better see that taking on the lordship of Christ means stopping publication of my magazine or completely changing its nature. If I am a manipulative politician, I will see that the lordship of Christ means that I no longer leave people twisting slowly in the wind. "Well," we may say, "who couldn't see these things? People are not without any integrity, you know." Granted, but people are immensely self-deceived. Clearly the rich young man had integrity, yet he had no firm grasp on his real problem. He had compromised for the sake of mammon so long that he no longer even considered himself to be compromising. Jesus had to spell out the compromise in bold letters to get him to see the truth. So it is with most of us. We need things spelled out for us. Mass, impersonal formulas may result in lengthy membership rolls, but they will definitely not produce hardcore disciples of Christ.

Jesus and Two from the Religious Hierarchy

When we think of Jesus in relation to the religious hierarchy of his day, we tend to think of his opposition to and denunciation of the hierarchy. Opposition and denunciation we surely find in Jesus, yet we do not find a rigid categorization of people. Jesus did not put people in a box. We must note, for example, that Nicodemus was a Pharisee and also a member of the ruling council, the Sanhedrin. He was a person of intense religious concern who presumably became a disciple of Jesus. Joseph of Arimathea, the man who, along with Nicodemus, prepared Jesus' body for burial and placed it in his newly made tomb, was also a member of the Sanhedrin.

Many of the religious hierarchy, especially the scribes and Pharisees, were earnest in their religious search. Although the religion of the day tended to emphasize externals and the basics of the law were often buried under a mountain of minutia, many still had not lost their way in the labyrinth of legalism.

The lawyer who came to test Jesus with questions about eternal life (Luke 10:25-37) was one who had not lost his way. He was on target with respect to the law. "What does the law say about achieving eternal life?" Jesus asked. The lawyer replied by citing the two great commandments: Love God and love your neighbor. Jesus commended him for his insight and then went on to clarify neighbor love by telling the parable of the good Samaritan. After telling the parable, he turned to the lawyer and said, "Go and do likewise." These are words directed at an honest inquirer. Exactly what Jesus intended we cannot say. Perhaps the lawyer thought, as did the rich young man, that he was adequately adhering to God's law. Jesus' parable was enough to relieve him of any such thought. At any rate, the lawyer was not categorized and dismissed simply as a hypocrite. Jesus dealt with him as an individual, a seeker serious in his inquiry about eternal life.

The scribe who asked Jesus which was the first commandment (Mark 12:28-34) was treated similarly. The question indicated that the scribe had a sense of priorities. He apparently did not buy the brand of legalism that leveled the commands of God to one plane, making all equally authoritative and binding. One might admit that all God's commands are equally authoritative, but to say that all are equally binding in the sense of being equally important and equally worthy of our attention and energy requires a great leap in logic. Theoretically, no rabbi of any consequence would have denied that some commands—in particular, the *shema* (Deuteronomy 6:4)—were more important than others. The problem came in practical application, in what received attention in teaching and personal conduct.

The phenomenon of legalism continues to flourish throughout religion in America, especially in groups that have developed specific measures of "holiness." All the groups would undoubtedly grant that the most important commands are to love God and one's neighbor. Yet the emphasis in preaching, teaching, and practice may betray a different set of priorities. Thus, the person who says "damn" or "hell" is often viewed as seriously deficient in the faith, regardless of how earnestly he seeks God, how honestly she conducts her business, how sensitive and caring he is for his family, or how involved she is in projects of compassion and care. He or she said, "_____" and so is suspect as a Christian. It follows in such circles that the person who has pure language is a better Christian. We are reminded of the words of Jesus to the scribes and Pharisees: "You tithe mint and dill and cummin, and have neglected the weightier matters of the law, justice and mercy and faith. . . . You blind guides, straining out a gnat and swallowing a camel!" (Matthew 23:23-24).

However, the scribe who questioned Jesus was not "straining out a gnat." When Jesus replied to his question about the great commandment by citing the *shema* and then the law of neighbor-love, the scribe in his turn responded by saying that Jesus was most certainly correct, that truly no other commandments take precedence over the two cited by Jesus. Jesus, perceiving the insight and sincerity of the scribe, said in commendation: "You are not far from the kingdom of God" (Mark 12:34). Again, the full and exact meaning of Jesus' words here is not clear. What was the scribe lacking? We cannot be certain, but the scribe was entirely on target in his perception of the central values of the kingdom. Jesus commended him personally for this keen perception. These words of commendation may have functioned as a spur to further inquiry concerning the kingdom.

Conclusion

As we reflect on the personal treatment accorded to people by Jesus, we cannot but reflect on the impersonal treatment we experience daily. An inescapable impersonal maze that continually frustrates us is the bureaucratic maze, a maze we confront not only in government but also in education, business, and the church. We are told that the rules say thus and so, and that, as a consequence, nothing can be done about our problem. Or we are told that action cannot be taken until some committee meets. In short, we are told that rules and procedures are more important than the people being served. To be sure, the rules and procedures were developed ostensibly to assure fairness and avoid favoritism; yet a rigid, inflexible adherence to rules and procedures can be unfair or even inhumane. In the real world of human affairs exceptions occur regularly. Rules or procedures that fail to make provision for exceptions are rules or procedures that fail to achieve fairness or humane service. Parents are fully aware that their children require different treatment according to their different personalities and needs. To dole out to each child exactly the same portion of time or attention would be to slight one and favor another. Thus, truly fair and humane rules and procedures will take into account the individual situations of persons.

Nancy had to get a tuberculosis test in order to teach. She could get to the county clinic, which was fifteen miles from her school, only during her lunch hour and period break. On the first day of class she rushed over to the clinic, only to find that it was closed during the lunch hour. "Typical government service, or nonservice," she thought. But she decided to wait. With luck she could zip through and get back to school in time for her fifth period class. Luck was not on her side. The clinic personnel returned from lunch late, the line moved at a slow crawl, and when Nancy did reach the clerk, she was authoritatively informed that she must have a card signed by her principal.

"Well, give me the card and I'll get it signed," Nancy said. "But let me get my test now. You only give the test from 10-3:30, excluding the lunch hour, and I teach until 3:20. I'll drop off the card on my way home."

"I'm sorry, lady," came the reply, "but you have to have the card signed first."

"I understand that I have to get the card signed. I'll do that."

"You must get the card signed first. That's the rule."

"May I speak with the supervisor, please?" Nancy asked.

"The supervisor is still out for lunch. Besides, she'd tell you exactly what I have."

Nancy left in frustration. Rules could not be adjusted to personal circumstances, even though doing so would have been functional, humane, and certainly not unfair.

We have all had Nancy-type experiences and we do not appreciate them. We want to be treated as individuals, not as an average or typical person, an intake unit, a number, a series of holes on a card. Whereas the politician may crow about the decrease of half a percentage point in unemployment, I may not see anything to crow about because unemployment where I live is eight points above the national norm. More importantly, I may have been without work for six months. However, many politicians love to concentrate on impersonal statistics, rather than on the individuals who do not fit the statistical pattern.

However we may be treated in society, we want to be treated as individuals. To want to be so treated is to be aware of our self-worth. We are worth being recognized individually. Those who doubt their self-worth will only have their doubts intensified by impersonal treatment. On the other hand, a good dose of personal treatment will go a long way toward curing self-doubts.

Grant, who wasn't too secure in himself, came home from the party simply walking on air. "Well, what was so great about the party?" his father asked.

"They had a neat band and great food, and all the kids were there," Grant answered. What he didn't tell his father was what really made the evening great. Tony, the student body president, talked a straight twenty minutes with Grant. Not only that, Grant danced with Tony's girl friend, and she really seemed to enjoy herself. No wonder Grant was pleased with himself.

Since we are worth something, we simply cannot and do not want to relate to those who do not recognize our worth, who are not interested in us for who we are. Those who put us in a box, who categorize us as a prospective client or voter or buyer or church member are just not the kinds of persons to whom we can be interested in relating. They are thing-persons, not people-persons. To relate is to share life; but to share our life a person must be interested in us, in our feelings, our emotions, our doubts, our fears, our thoughts, our hopes, our plans, our frustrations, our successes. A person may not especially like to hear some of the things we want to share—our fears and frustrations—but if that person is really interested in us, he or she will listen.

Impersonal treatment seems to be increasing geometrically in North America. The increase seems to be directly linked, at least to the lay mind, to the computer. The computer can improve the quality of life, making it more humane in many ways. In other ways, though, the computer does depersonalize. Consider the checkout stand at the supermarket. In many stores we no longer hear the checker's voice; we hear an artificial voice from a program disk. Even though we may want and need to be addressed by another human being, we do not get what we want and need except by superhuman effort. Undoubtedly the program cuts down on checker errors; yet sometimes our response is, "So what?"

The children of the kingdom are people who live in the world—the world of computers, robots, mass production, mass media, mass bureaucracy—but they are not of this world; they do not buy into the impersonal systems and procedures. They may be computer or robotic experts, but they do not treat others as computers or robots, and they fight depersonalizing policies or procedures that may be associated with these machines. In short, the children of the kingdom are person-centered, as was Jesus, focusing on the individual in all of his or her concrete uniqueness. They are followers of their Master, who always kept his eye on the individual.

6

Jesus and Plain Speaking

Clay was head of research programs at the university. He was a fine scholar and had been placed in a respected administrative position because of his research skills. However, Clay didn't have the faintest notion how to administer a research program or anything else. The result was confusion, mishandling of funds, arbitrariness in issuing grants, and so on. An audit of the research department revealed that $1,500 was missing. The president of the university issued a statement that Clay would remain in his position, that he had full confidene in Clay, that the problems in the research department were minor and had, in fact, already been straightened out.

A letter of resignation from Clay surfaced a month later. The president issued a statement of regret, saying that the resignation had nothing to do with the missing $1,500.

These days the story of Clay is far from a novelty. The thought of firing anybody outright is anathema, in business and government as well as in education. People are not fired; they resign.

One of the few persons of national consequence in recent history to be fired was Lee Iacocca, from Ford Motor Company. (Perhaps being fired had something to do with

Iacocca's role in the spectacular turnaround of Chrysler.) In one sense Ford's action was refreshing. There was no shuffling with the truth; no euphemisms; no rhetoric. Iacocca was fired, period.

One wonders whom the executives think they are kidding when they keep talking about resignation. The only people fooled are those issuing the palpably false statements.

Regrettably, our society is flooded with falsehoods and euphemisms. The MX missile, a missile undeniably offensive in nature, is called the "Peacekeeper." The pullout of the marines in Lebanon was a "redeployment of the troops" to the offshore ships. The contras in Nicaragua are being supported in order to "disrupt the flow of arms to El Salvador," except that the evidence for a *flow* of arms is sparse at best. Taxes are not taxes but "revenue enhancers." Olympic athletes are "amateurs" even though they may live from the income of trust funds of six or seven figures. The advertising campaign for Ford Motor Company in 1984 focused on the theme "We build quality cars," even though the previous year Ford had the second highest recall for cars among both domestic and foreign car manufacturers.

To be sure, we go through phases during which truthfulness and speaking forthrightly are emphasized, at least by certain segments of our society. Thus, the children of the sixties talked about "letting it all hang out," and in the seventies we heard much about "telling it like it is." We get fed up with the coverup, euphemism, and falsehood, and the pendulum begins to swing in the other direction; but before long we're back to business as usual.

For Jesus the usual business was the business of the kingdom, the business of letting a yes be yes and a no be no, the business of saying what needed to be said, even though doing so may have been less than flattering or less than pleasant to the hearer.

The hard truth often comes as a burden or as a blow from a hammer; yet Jesus was not one to avoid articulating the hard truth. Jesus condemned the myopia and hypocrisy of large portions of the religious hierarchy; he rebuked Peter severely; he told Martha bluntly that she was too preoccupied with domestic affairs. Jesus was not one to make a point indirectly. He was direct and plainspoken.

Jesus and Mary

At the beginning of his ministry Jesus and the apostles went to a wedding party (John 2:1-11). Although Jesus was to be about the business of redemption, he was clearly not a morose person. Indeed, he contrasted himself to John the Baptist, saying that whereas John came as an ascetic, fasting and living in the desert,[1] he came eating and drinking, living in normal society (Matthew 11:18-19).

At the wedding party Jesus undoubtedly joined in celebrating with the rest of the guests. A large wedding celebration often made a considerable dent in the provisions of food and drink; in fact, at this party the wine ran out. Jesus' mother, upon hearing of the disastrous shortfall, immediately came to Jesus, saying, "The wine has run out." We may presume that she was not just passing on information to Jesus but was, in effect, indirectly telling him what to do. Jesus' reply to her was; "O woman, what have you to do with me? My time has not yet come" (John 2:4). The reply must have brought his mother up short. Yet she absolutely had to understand, and understand immediately, that she was to have nothing to do with Jesus' mission and ministry. She was not to try to direct him concerning the use of miracle. Jesus had received no divine guidance about the wine and would not act unless and until he did.

If Jesus' words to his mother seem harsh and unkind, we simply have to recall similar words which we may have spoken. Many parents continue to play their role with an adult son or daughter, issuing instructions or advice as if the offspring were still a child. Many adult children have had to say: "I am no longer your little child. I am an adult, capable of making my own decisions and running my own family. I would appreciate your recognizing this fact." Tough words, to be sure, but they are often necessary.

Apparently Jesus' tough words did not thoroughly penetrate his mother's mind, for we read that early in his ministry she, along with his brothers, came to take him home because they thought he had lost his senses (Mark 3:21, 31-35). When they arrived at the house where Jesus was, they could not get in because of the crowd. So they told the people to pass the message to Jesus that his mother and brothers were outside asking for him. Jesus' reply, which, if it was not heard by his mother and brothers, was surely passed on to them, was that his mother and brothers are those who do the will of God, those who listen to his teachings and act on them (v. 35). Jesus put the point in very extreme language on another occasion: "If any one comes to me and does not hate his own father and mother and wife and children and brothers and sisters, yes, and even his own life, he cannot be my disciple" (Luke 14:26). Perhaps the words of Jesus from Luke need further clarification. Aren't they really paradoxical? How can we on the one hand promote loving relationships with others and then say we should sacrifice this closeness for divine mission?

The paradox is only on the surface. Jesus, consistent with the teaching of the Jewish Scriptures, emphatically taught that the pursuit of God and relationship with God were the supreme objectives of humankind. If these objectives came into conflict with relationships to others, then those relationships would lose out. When would such a conflict be likely to arise? It would be likely to arise when somebody, perhaps a family member, opposed a person's pursuit of and commitment to God and did so by means other than discussion, argument, and rational persuasion. Given a mature person who is totally committed to the God of biblical faith, we would have to say that those who require a person to choose between that person and his or her religion are imposing an improper requirement, a requirement which goes far beyond the rights of any relationship. To fail to respect another's freedom, to try to manipulate and control another, is to undercut a relationship at its most fundamental level.

Jesus, then, unambiguously asserted that the pursuit of God takes precedence over relationships with others. Jesus' family, including his mother, had not accepted this truth in practice, although they undoubtedly accepted it theoretically inasmuch as it was basic to the Jewish religion. Jesus merely reminded them of their own primary commitment.

Jesus and Nicodemus

Nicodemus came to Jesus at night presumably to avoid detection (John 3:1-16). He began the conversation with Jesus by engaging in some low-level flattery: "Rabbi, we know that you are a teacher come from God" (v. 2). In referring to "we," Nicodemus certainly did not mean the religious hierarchy; they gave little evidence of seeing Jesus as a teacher from God. Indeed, the religious hierarchy in general was unsympathetic to Jesus from the very beginning of his ministry, many being so hostile they wished to kill Jesus immediately (Mark 3:6). So Jesus brushed aside the remark of Nicodemus. Jesus was no after-dinner speaker needing a flowery introduction. He was on serious business: to seek and save the lost, including Nicodemus. Jesus addressed the problem squarely. "Nicodemus," he said, "you must be born from above. In spite of your religious status, you are not living in the world of God's kingdom. You need to enter that world. You need to be born from above" (vv. 5-7).

Nicodemus was used to flattery, to compliments, to pats on the back, to being addressed as "your eminence," "honored member of the Sanhedrin," and "devoted keeper of the law." But now this rabbi from Nazareth says unflatteringly: "You must be born again, born from above. Your

Abrahamic lineage is of no value whatsoever. Your religious status and accomplishments count for nothing in the kingdom of God. What counts is a radical new value reorientation to God and others. Are you willing to let God's Spirit blow away the refuse of your religiosity and blow into you the life of God?"

Jesus' pointed words presented Nicodemus with an unmistakable choice. There was no question, no ambiguity, about where Nicodemus stood and where he needed to stand, about where he was and where he needed to go. Jesus pierced through the crust of convention in order to focus Nicodemus's mind on his real spiritual condition. In doing so, Jesus was also dealing with Nicodemus in a very personal way. He was confronting the specific need of Nicodemus as a Pharisee, using language that would immediately get his attention. "You must be born again, born from above." Jesus is not reported to have used this language anywhere else; yet it was perfect for Nicodemus. What could shock him into his religious senses more effectively than a statment to the effect that he was not even a beginner in the kingdom? The statement surely spoke to him, and Nicodemus entered the kingdom.

Jesus and the Syrophoenician Woman

A story that we normally do not relish studying is that of the Syrophoenician woman (Mark 7:24-30). The reason we shy away from the story is that it seems to represent Jesus as prejudiced. Jesus spoke to the Syrophoenician woman in a way that simply cries out for explanation.

The woman came asking Jesus to cast a demon out of her daughter. Jesus' incredible reply was: "Let the children first be fed, for it is not right to take the children's bread and throw it to the dogs (v. 27). This blunt statement seems to reveal terrible prejudice. Or does it?

The place to begin an analysis of Jesus' statement is with other stories relating Jesus' treatment of Gentiles. Unfortunately, there are not many such stories, for Jesus' first mission was to the Jews, an idea certainly latent in his words to the woman. However, in the case of the Roman centurion whose servant was healed by Jesus (Matthew 8:5-13) nothing whatsoever is said about the exclusion of Gentiles from the ministry of Jesus. In fact, Jesus said that many Gentiles would sit at table in the kingdom, whereas many Jews would not. Moreover, the centurion and the Syrophoenician woman were surely not the only Gentiles seeking healing from Jesus. We read nowhere else in the Gospels of anyone being rejected for healing because he or she was a Gentile. Further, the story of the good Samaritan was hardly accidentally developed. Jesus' choice of a Samaritan to illustrate neighbor-love was clearly a rebuke of Jewish prejudice, which suggested that Samaritans were no better than Gentiles; indeed, they were worse because they engaged in what the Jew viewed as a perverted form of Jehovah worship. We could cite other instances of Jesus' acceptance of and lack of prejudice toward Gentiles. Therefore, the Syrophoenician woman probably represented a special case. Jesus' blunt words must have been a way of getting to an individual problem that Jesus perceived. Thus, the story reveals not only Jesus' plain-spokenness but also the individual nature of his approach.

What was the problem Jesus addressed? Here we are reduced to speculation. The woman may well have been deeply prejudiced herself. To Jewish exclusivism she may have reacted with a virulent exclusivism of her own. Jesus' words would have immediately fingered the nerve of her exclusivism, or perhaps Jesus was testing her persistence and faith. Throughout the Gospels we read of Jesus' commendation of persistence (e.g., Luke 11:5-10; 18:1-8). Indeed, true faith reveals itself in a persistence of purpose that pursues its object even through a labyrinth of obstacles. Jesus was after people with a seriousness of purpose. So when Jesus found the woman's faith to be of the "blue ribbon" variety, he commended her with the words: "O woman, great is your faith."

Conclusion

We can characterize American society in a number of ways—for example, as the hula-hoop society, to indicate our devotion to fads. Of greater relevance to our purpose, we could characterize American society as the memo society. Memos are generated for everything necessary and unnecessary. Sometimes a memo performs a necessary informative role. Too often, however, the memo is a cover for a weak executive. Somebody has gotten out of line, abused a rule or privilege. Instead of confronting that somebody directly, a memo is circulated, stating the problem and the relevant rule—or revoking a privilege. A memo is a strictly impersonal method of communication. The way to avoid closeness with a person is to avoid face-to-face relationships. A memo avoids face-to-face relationships. In doing so, it indicates a lack of courage on the part of the sender, a lack of courage to confront a problem directly and deal with a person one on one. As a result, a memo is often an ineffective way to handle a problem.

What is behind the lack of courage that prompts so many memos? Why would a person be so lacking in courage, in inner strength, that he or she would take the circuitous, indirect, and ineffective route of the memo? A shaky sense of self-worth is one clear answer. Direct confrontation risks the reaction of hostility, defensiveness, and return criticism. If we are not secure about ourselves, we shall be hesitant about receiving a barrage of negative feelings and statements from another. Yet resolving problems effectively calls for the willingness to risk such barrages.

Naturally, there are people who make a practice of "chewing out" others, often in front of an audience. They may pride themselves on their directness, their plainspokenness, their toughness, but they are really afflicted with a weak sense of self-worth (as are people with "memo-syndrome"). In short, they suffer from the "put-down syndrome," a condition that shouts of a severely damaged sense of self-worth.

Plainspokenness, then, is not a virtue in and of itself; it is of value only in the proper context and only when proceeding from proper motives. Plainspokenness is not appropriate in every set of circumstances. Admittedly, being plainspoken is a form of being honest and up-front with a person. However, sharing feelings and thoughts, especially negative ones, must always be conditioned by a sense of proportion. We need to tread the path of reasonability. If we unload on people what they are in no condition to receive, we are not acting in a loving way. To care for another deeply is to find out how a person is feeling and act accordingly.

Another guiding principle of plainspokenness is the identification of problems in order to resolve them. To be sure, we may speak plainly even though we know that our words will fall on deaf ears and unresponsive hearts. Granted, the truth sometimes must be enunciated regardless of the response. The ministry of Jesus was hardly one grand success story during his lifetime. Nevertheless, it is important to consider the effectiveness of our words. Thus, we do not constantly remind a person of a disability, although doing so would be a matter of stating the truth plainly, because no purpose would be served thereby. Similarly, nagging is not a recommended course because it is ineffective, if not counterproductive. The fundamental reason for being plainspoken is to raise to consciousness that which is not clearly in the conscious. The rich young ruler, for example, was not fully aware of how much he cherished his wealth; he was self-deceived. He had willfully subverted his soul and obscured the clarity of his consciousness; therefore, Jesus had to penetrate the mists and to raise to the sunlight of awareness the young man's true value commitments. Having done so, however, Jesus could do little more. What would additional pointed words accomplish? The young man went away sorrowfully, but Jesus could say no more. When Jesus sent out the apostles to deliver the message of the kingdom, they were told to leave those cities that would not receive their message, shaking off the dust of the streets from their sandals (Mark 6:7-13). What is the use of harping on the Gospel when doing so is clearly ineffective? Jesus put the point bluntly when he said: "Do not throw your pearls before the swine" (Matthew 7:6).

Effectiveness is a fundamental consideration in plain-spokenness; further, effectiveness is largely a function of care. Persons who care do not just slash and tear. Their aim is to accomplish something useful or helpful or to remind others of essential truth.

Stuart was terminally ill with cancer. Yet he and his wife, Mildred, had never talked about his condition since they learned of its gravity. Incredibly enough, they consistently managed to skirt even the word "cancer."

One day, their friends Betty and Ward visited Stuart in the hospital. Mildred was there, too. The conversation started pleasantly enough, and then Betty began talking about cancer. Betty always said just what was on her mind, no matter how outrageous. At least that's what her friends continually told her. Actually her frankness was often the source of great humor at parties. Now here was Betty talking to Stuart about her cancer. She was at a serious stage of cancer herself. Then she talked about Stuart's cancer. Mildred's eyes widened. But then Stuart started talking about his cancer; and finally, Mildred, ever so timidly, used the word once . . . twice. . . .

At the end of the visit Mildred, with tears in her eyes, said, "We've never been able to talk like this until now. Thank you. Thank you for your visit." Ward prayed then and could hardly get Stuart to let go of his hand when he finished.

What happened? Why was Betty so effective with Stuart and Mildred and others? Betty cared and her caring simply could not be cloaked. Her frankness continually came on the wings of care, with the result that she genuinely ministered to people.

Although plainspokenness is often necessary and useful, we generally avoid it in superficial relationships, in our normal business and social contacts. We do not wish to expend our energy on what really does not matter to us, with the result that we resort to half-truths and euphemisms. Yet sacrificing the truth requires a better justification than unwillingness to expend energy on what we do not think is important. Sacrificing the truth requires better justification than the facile statement "Oh, I didn't want to hurt him." If a person performs abysmally in his job, he or she knows that and knows that everybody else knows. Dancing around the truth by saying that one resigned, rather than that one was fired, will not ease the pain. In fact, the person might be forced to do a bit of reevaluation. "What am I really after? Wealth? Power? Maybe I ought to be after something else." Being forthright may also lead to better choices on the part of management in the future.

In any case, truth is not something with which we can play. Jesus said, "Let your yes be yes and your no, no" (Matthew 5:37). To speak the truth is to respect one's humanity; it is to see one as a person of worth and dignity, a being made in God's image, deserving and having a right to the truth. Who, for instance, would speak falsehoods before God? To do so would be an affront to the greatness and glory of God. Thus, to fail to speak the truth is an affront to one as a being made in God's image. Even though the truth may be difficult for the hearer to receive, stating it shows a deep respect for and a clear sense of the hearer's dignity.

Although we are under the obligation of truth to all persons, we normally reserve plainspokenness—at least the plainspokenness that goes beyond our obligation of truth—for those who are close to us. For those who are close to us, plainspokenness is a way of saying, "You and I have a good enough relationship that we can be open and frank. Ours is no fragile relationship; it is a relationship of considerable toughness." But it may be that the value of loving relationships requires the risk of plainspokenness with many more persons than those with whom we are comfortable.

7

The Kingdom, Culture, and Persons

To conclude our discussion of Jesus and personal relations, we shall turn first to a strange, even bizarre, incident in the life of Jesus, the incident concerning the healing of the demoniac and the drowning of the swine (Mark 5:1-20).

Jesus and the apostles had pulled their boat up on the eastern shore of the Sea of Galilee when they heard inhuman screams and shrieks in the distance. Looking up, they saw a man racing toward them. He was naked, a powerfully built man, as fierce looking as a lion. Peter immediately put his hand to the hilt of his sword, but Jesus shook his head. Peter's reaction was to handle this demoniac with force, violence. In fact, the townspeople had followed that logic but to little avail. Every time they attempted to control the man forcefully, he simply burst free with Samson-like displays of strength. The man was a threat to life and property and, they thought, had to be removed from town. Removing him had not been a great problem, though, for one morning he had gone on his own to live in the tombs near the seashore.

The man had lived in the tombs for many years, an outcast from society. Young boys would sometimes venture out to torment the "crazy man." But the moment he took a few steps in their direction they would, of course, take off toward home.

Now the outcast was at Jesus' feet, screaming that Jesus should not torment him. Jesus looked at him with compassion and asked: "What is your name?"

Here was an approach completely sensitive to the man's need. Yes, his name, for he perceived himself as a legion, as a multiplicity of beings. What could bring back unity to such a fractured self? Or what could restore the man's sense of autonomy and authority over his own soul? "What is your name?" was a call back to reality.

"My name is Legion." The man resisted the call. But then he said: "Send us into the swine" (v. 12). He was willing to come back to himself; he wanted his individuality back; he wanted autonomy, reality, wholeness. Jesus told Legion to depart into the swine and never return to the man again. As the disciples looked on with gaping mouths, the herd of swine began to move. Despite the swineherds' efforts, the herd gained momentum and ran straight over the enbankment into the sea. After a few moments of thrashing and squealing, the herd became nothing but a motionless mass in the choppy waters of the sea. The man was healed, but the townspeople were not concerned with the man. They considered the material loss greater than the human gain. "Jesus," they said, "you are too risky, too costly to have around. Yes, the crazy man is sane again. That's fine! But please go away, Jesus!" These people revealed the chasm between themselves and the kingdom, between the value of things and the value of persons. Who really had the demons?

The pursuit of kingdom values is likely to be costly for us in our profit-motivated society. This is not to say that all segments of our society ignore human values. There are personal, people-oriented policies in business as well as in government, education, and other areas of our society.

A recent study by Thomas J. Peters and Robert H. Waterman, Jr., focuses on a sample of forty-three companies that met a series of criteria for excellence and positve performance over a twenty-year period. The companies are large ones, with annual sales in the one-billion-dollar range and above. Peters and Waterman discovered, among other things, that the companies were people-oriented. They respected the individuality and creativity of their employees as well as the desires and needs of their customers. As a result of their study, Peters and Waterman come down hard on what they call the numerative, rationalist approach to management, the approach which, they say, dominates U. S. business schools. The idea of this approach is that a well-trained manager can handle anything as long as he employs a detached, analytical, rationally hardheaded method. The problem with this method, say Peters and Waterman, is that the approach is really irrational. It sees persons as playing pieces on a game board, rather than as individuals with creative minds, feelings, imaginations, ambitions, and beliefs.

Peters and Waterman cite Hewlett-Packard as an outstanding example of a people-oriented company. They provide the following statement from Bill Hewlett.

'I feel that it [the HP way] is the policies and actions that flow from the belief that men and women want to do a good job, a creative job, and that if they are provided with the proper environment they will do so. It is the tradition of treating every individual with consideration and respect and recognizing personal achievements. This sounds almost trite, but Dave [cofounder Packard] and I honestly believe in this philosophy. . . . The dignity and worth of the individual is a very important part, then, of the HP Way. With this in mind, many years ago we did away with time clocks, and more recently we introduced the flexible work hours program. Again, this is meant to be an expression of trust and confidence in people as well as providing them with an opportunity to adjust their work schedules to their personal lives.[1]

Perhaps some of what Hewlett says is just old-fashioned

hype and perhaps some of his employees would write off his remarks as pure rhetoric; however, Peters and Waterman became believers. In any case, we can take Hewlett's statement as an expression of an ideal, an ideal thoroughly consistent with kingdom values.

Yet for every Hewlett-Packard there are many companies that never give the slightest consideration in policy or practice to human worth, welfare, or dignity. Some companies have little concern for human health or safety; rather, they have as much concern as the government makes them have.

Recently there was an article in a local paper about a reservoir regularly used by fisherman and swimmers but thoroughly polluted. The owner of the reservoir permitted area chemical companies to dump wastes in trenches on the reservoir levees for as little as ten dollars a load. The state is presently requesting the Environmental Protection Agency to add the site to its list of the worst waste dumps in the nation, thus making it eligible for clean-up funds. The questions arises: What should a child of the kingdom do when he or she is an employee of a company engaged in harmful dumping practices? "Blowing the whistle" could mean sacrificing a job or even a career. Perhaps the townspeople who asked Jesus to leave were not so morally perverse after all. Perhaps they were, but no more so than we who continually opt for economic values over kingdom values.

Consider another practice. Any number of pipeline and tank construction companies regularly fake or fraudulently manipulate X rays that show the strength of welds. The welders know of the practice; the supervisors know of it; and the owners or top managers know of it. Moreover, many of the welders, supervisors, and owners or managers regularly attend church; yet the fraudulent, illegal, harmful practice continues.

Consider what happens in times of recession. The normal policy for United States companies is to cut costs by laying off people, starting with the hourly workers. Undeniably, costs must be cut, but why must those least able to bear economic hardship shoulder the main burden? Peters and Waterman found that the companies achieving excellence had top-level staffs that were lean. The implication is that many other companies are bloated with upper-level staff and management. Yet when cutting takes place, it starts at the lowest levels or is toughest on the lowest levels.

Consider issues that are international in scope, issues such as arms sales to developing countries or investments in countries such as South Africa. These issues are controversial; however, the problem is that the issues normally are not even discussed, except by theologians who do not have the slightest connection with the boardrooms of power. As for the decision makers, their focus is often on only one item—profit. To complicate the clear issue of profit with questions about human rights or war and peace is simply to muddy the waters. Even raising the question of honesty may be considered something strictly for the Sunday-meeting crowd. If there is a bribe to pay to an international broker, pay it! Just keep the matter quiet and write if off as a business expense. Besides, if we don't pay the "fee," someone else will. How could we compete with other companies if we had unrealistic scruples about honesty or about human rights or about what other countries do with the arms we sell them?

The list of practices conflicting with kingdom values could go on. The point is that living by kingdom values in our society, in our cultural context, is a task of immense proportions. In other societies the task may be more or less immense. Yet the task in our society is large enough for any one of us, reaching from international issues to issues concerning personal lifestyle.

For example, our culture emphasizes the values of wealth and success. So why shouldn't we enjoy the symbols of wealth and success? Are these ostentatious symbols consistent with our kingdom commitment? "Well, no, but what is ostentation? I'm a multimillionaire, so is driving this fancy sports car ostentatious for me?"

"Maybe. I can't say, but you ought to think about it. Why not drive a modest car? I mean, what sort of image should a follower of Jesus project?"

"Oh, come off it."

"No, seriously, are you really attached to fancy cars and to the symbolism of wealth and status associated with them?"

And so the conversation could continue. The problem is that our culture does not encourage us to question our lifestyles; indeed, questioning is positively discouraged. The questions will arise only if we are clear about the demands of the kingdom and are attempting to respond to them in our lives.

A serious pursuit of the demands of the kingdom would, in the case of the values of wealth and success, quickly lead us past the issue of ostentation to the deeper issue of detachment. We have noted several times the fundamental role of detachment in the life of the disciples of Jesus. "You cannot serve God and mammon" (Matthew 6:24). To this verse our culture responds by saying, in effect: "Well, if that's the case, serve mammon!"—and with tragic results.

In the spring of 1985 farmers in the Midwest were going bankrupt in record numbers. David Stockman, then national director of the budget, voiced the opinion that the financial problems of the farmers were self-made, arising from simple over-expansion. His solution was to let the farmers bear the effects of their poor decisions. Since we live in a free-market economy, in which people are free to fail as well as succeed, those who fail should receive no special treatment. Many farmers went bankrupt. One farmer, after anguishing for months over his debt-burdened farm and seeing no way out of his debts, killed himself. He had many friends who had gone the second mile supporting him and his family in their time of crisis.

Yet he still took his own life. We surely do not know all the reasons why; however, his wife was reported as saying, "He just couldn't face losing so many things he loved, his very identity."[2] Unquestionably, land on which one has lived from childhood, a home, and a way of life ingrained in one's earliest memories cannot be easily shucked or reduced to the pursuit of mammon. Of course, Jesus' words about mammon should not be interpreted simplistically as referring only to money. Jesus was talking about material things generally and the way of life associated with the pursuit of and attachment to material things. (See the entire passage, Matthew 6:24-34.)

In another instance, the workers at a Texas oil drilling company thought that they had become rich. Before his death the owner of the company had arranged for his workers to become shareholders in the company. When the company went public in 1981 the workers were offered a payoff on their interest in the company, an average of about $500,000 a worker. Most workers opted to take the payoff in company stock, which had been soaring in value. Then the recession of the early 1980s hit and the stock depreciated to practically nothing. Unfortunately, most workers had borrowed against the original value of the stock. Thus, the workers were in financial trouble. One man said: "It's ruined me. I've been thinking about suicide, bankruptcy—all sorts of things." This man had, unhappily , hitched his wagon to the mammon star. When it crashed, he was ruined. Yet what sort of lifestyle leaves one ruined when the mammon star crashes? Can the crash take away friends, loved ones, sharing, closeness, affection, acceptance? Another man had this perspective: "All I know is that I'm not too worried about anybody taking anything from me. I didn't have nothin' before this stock and I still don't have nothin'. And nothin' from nothin' is nothin'."[3] Actually, this man had plenty. He had values that sustained him in a time of loss and thjerefore did not see himself as ruined.

Detachment from things, attachment to persons—this is the way of the kingdom; and it should be the core message and example of the church. Unfortunately, the church too often gets drawn into the whirlpool of cultural values and the message of the kingdom is drowned.

The headlines in the religion section of the newspaper read "Growth: Nothing Succeeds like Success." The article was based on an interview with the pastor of a rapidly growing church in an affluent section of one of our large cities. The article stressed that the church, which is practically homogeneous, is the third largest of its denomination in the city and is continuing to grow in numbers. Further, the church had just completed a multimillion dollar expansion, which made it "competitive in facilities" with the largest church. Why was this church growing? Said the pastor: "The people of this city are winners, and they want to be a part of a winning team." (Not exactly a biblical thought!) Numerical growth, plant expansion, budget growth—these mark what is called a successful church as well as a successful business. The pastor who has these marks on a resumé is assured of moving up, as would be any executive in the corporate world.

What do any of these marks of success have to do with kingdom values? Put differently, what do these cultural measures of success have to do with kingdom measures of success? Several years ago I visited one of the congregational units of the Church of the Savior in Washington, D.C. The group met on a Monday night in an old building located in a low-income section of the city. About fifty people were present, representing a broad spectrum of racial/ethnic groups and social classes. We met around tables, singing, praying, sharing Communion, and partaking a common supper. Although a stranger, I felt an atmosphere of warmth and closeness. I shall never forget the words of one woman, who had just committed herself to membership in the church. "Christ is people—right?" For her, Christ was the people of that Christian community, people who took her into one of the community-owned apartments when she was without housing, people who helped her obtain a job through their employment center, and people who offered her medical services through their clinic. She would have to go through a fairly lengthy period of training, study, and service before she would be received into full membership, and she was committed to do so. She said nothing about wanting to be on a winning team. What she wanted—and what she had—was a small, close, creative, caring community of fellow strugglers.

The "growing" church is, of course, far more representative of the North American church than the small, caring church. The former is not lacking totally in kingdom values, for a closer examination of the church would reveal that it is helping some people find the narrow path of a serious search for God and for loving relationships with others. Unquestionably, though, the church in North America has let the cultural measures of success (more specifically, the cultural measures of corporate or business success) infect its life. The church has uncritically adopted these measures of success to evaluate its health, with the result that its health has been seriously compromised.

Certainly, the point here is not that the church and Christian people should go about announcing the intention to be failures. Instead, the point is that success as measured by our culture is often a universe away from success as measured by the value of loving relationships. The same is true for a whole list of other cultural values.

The North American church stands in desperate need of radical renewal and restructuring whereby every policy, every goal, every activity, every program, every interest is constantly measured against the values at the very core of the universe—the values of persons and loving relationships. Accomplishing this renewal and restructuring requires clarity of vision, tenacity in pursuing the vision, and the illumination and power of the Holy Spirit. In no other way can the church rise above "this evil age"—the culture of the world—to live by the culture of the kingdom, the culture of persons and loving relationships, the culture of the abundant life.

Discussion Questions

Chapter 1

1. What was the attitude of the early Christians toward the government of Rome? toward government generally? The early Christians appear to be apolitical. Were they really? What are the implications for political involvement for Christians today?

2. What are the differences between our cultural codes and customs on sex and violence and the values of the New Testament? Has the church yielded to the cultural values of sex and violence?

3. What other capacities besides communicating, making moral decisions, and self-consciousness distinguish men and women as persons?

4. On page 15, is the list of values likely to conflict with kingdom values complete? What would you add? Why?

5. What specific programs in your church are directed toward developing loving relationships? What programs

could be instituted in your church to bring about and enhance loving relationships?

6. What are some of the important activities that bring about self-growth?

7. Discuss in detail the requirements for keeping a relationship alive, interesting, and exciting.

8. How can we in the church help people achieve an image of God that is free of cultural bias?

9. What do John 7:17 and Romans 1:18 have to say about the reasons for our resistance to the truth?

10. What beliefs in your church tradition would you consider dogma, lacking in clear biblical support? What practices would you consider tradition? Are any of these beliefs or practices detrimental to biblical religion?

11. As part of the culture of the kingdom, what should we do about housing for the poor, for those on welfare or with marginal incomes? What plan would you recommend? What can your church do in your community?

Chapter 2

1. What are some common ways that women are exploited in our society? In what ways are they placed in an inferior position to men? Is there exploitation of women in the church? in your church? What may be done to straighten things out?

2. Why did not Jesus include women among his apostles? Does this show that Jesus shared some of the prejudices

of his contemporaries?

3. In your church are women given a status of equality with men? Is the status they are given justified by Scripture? Does Scripture support the idea of women serving in the clergy? What are the implications of Jesus' treatment of women?

4. What are some explanations for the Old Testament rules on cleanness and uncleanness?

5. Is disease ever a punishment for sin? Explain.

6. Discuss the statement: "I forgive but I don't forget." (See Isaiah 43:25; Jeremiah 31:34; Micah 7:18-20.)

7. How can the church be inclusive of all persons and at the same time let the world know that it takes sin seriously? When, if ever, are we justified in excluding people from the church?

Chapter 3

1. What do you think of the Greek view that the emotions should be under the control and guidance of reason? Is the view biblical? Explain.

2. In what ways may the expression of grief be a sign of strength?

3. What can your church do to assist people more adequately during their times of grief?

4. What does the verse in Ephesians 4:26 concerning anger mean?

5. What are some instances in which we, like the religious leaders who were after Jesus, develop excuses to justify moral abuse—abuses employed, perhaps, to maintain our positions of power, prestige, and wealth?

6. Do we have practices in the church that, like the practices in the temple of Jesus' day, smack of sheer commercialism? If so, note some of the practices. Are there any in your church?

7. In what ways can "honesty" in the case of emotions, i.e., always letting others know exactly how we feel, be harmful and detrimental? Do we have a moral obligation to be honest in this sense?

8. Are we correct in attributing emotions to God? Isn't doing this an instance of anthropomorphizing God? If we do not attribute emotions to God, what are the implications for relationship with God?

9. What are some ways to bring about constructive change in our emotions? How can we tap God's power to bring about change? What can the church do? your church?

10. Discuss whether or not fear and doubt in Jesus are consistent with the view of Jesus as the Son of God. What does the Bible indicate about fear and doubt in Jesus?

11. Is it really true that Christ's peace (John 14:27; 16:33) can eliminate all anxiety? Discuss.

12. Does your church or denomination have lifestyle standards that serve as a source of improper guilt? If so, what

are they? Aside from what has been mentioned already in the text, what are some common sources of improper guilt in our culture?

13. What can we do to help people (including ourselves) feel forgiven? What is your church doing? What can it do?

14. When we dislike someone, are we not really failing to accept that person? Is this sort of action ever justified? Are there levels of acceptance so that in some sense we may accept people we dislike? What sense would it be? Is it a biblical sense?

Chapter 4

1. Although human love that involves closeness and communion cannot be impartial, what can be said about divine love? If love involves desires, then how can God love?

2. What is usually the reason for immediate attraction to a person? Are any of the reasons sufficient for an enduring relationship? What is necessary in order to have an enduring relationship?

3. Some psychologists say that feelings often, if not always, follow or are determined by behavior. Have you found truth in this view? Explain.

4. When, if ever, is breaking a friendship relationship justified? How about a marriage relationship?

5. "Neighbor-love is impossible apart from self-love." Discuss. If we really love ourselves, what goals will we set for ourselves?

6. Do the moral obligations of Christians and non-Christians differ in any respects? For example, is a non-Christian under any obligation to forgive and accept others?

7. In seeking closeness, can we avoid the risks of vulnerability? What can we do to reduce the risks—or should we be concerned about doing so? How did Jesus model vulnerability?

8. If we are not constantly smiling or bubbling with joy, have we in some sense failed in our Christian lives? Discuss.

9. How can classing some emotions as male or female be a form of self-deception?

10. What do we reveal about ourselves by resorting to self-deception? In what ways does the church engage in or encourage self-deception? What can the church do to help people avoid self-deception?

Chapter 5

1. When we treat a person as a thing, what attributes are we denying to the person? What rights do we violate?

2. What is wrong with using the corporate model in education? Do we ever use the model in the church? Explain. If so, what are the consequences of using the corporate model in the church?

3. Although the electronic church essentially employs a nonindividualistic appeal, it still attracts masses of people. Why? In what sense is the electronic church a comment

on the adequacy of the local church?

4. Although a packaged, standardized, high-pressure approach to evangelism often "works," what are the weaknesses of the approach? How did Jesus do evangelism?

5. What are the practices of evangelism in your church? Are you reaching the unchurched? What new program or approaches would you suggest?

6. Peter's experience with the fish (Luke 5:1-11) impressed him with the extraordinary nature of Jesus. Relate an experience you have had that made you aware of the extraordinary nature of Jesus. In what sense do Christian witness and evangelism depend on personal experiences with Christ?

7. In what ways do we reveal ourselves to be as prideful as Peter? In what programs or practices do we normally engage without seriously seeking divine guidance and power?

8. Does leadership in the church require more than having been forgiven? Are the requirements for leadership in the church more than the requirements of acceptance and fellowship? Explain.

9. In what ways do church members hold one another at arms' length? What can your church do to bring people into closer contact, to develop New Testament "fellowship"? What would be the likely effects of New Testament fellowship on the unchurched?

10. The incident of Mary anointing Jesus at Bethany apparently triggered Judas's decision to betray Jesus. What are the possible reasons why the incident triggered his decision?

11. When are we to give up on people? Ever? How about Jesus' statement to move on to another town if not accepted in one town? Is moving on a form of giving up?

12. In contrast to the other religious leaders and teachers of the day, Jesus always seemed to draw a crowd. Why? Was is just because of his miracles or also because of other personality traits? If the latter, which traits?

13. Why do some people adopt their sickness as their way of life? What course of action should be taken toward these individuals?

14. What are some of the signs of our attachment to things? What command do you think Jesus would address to us? Would it be different from the command addressed to the rich young nobleman?

15. In what ways does the church use statistics in an impersonal way? How can this be avoided? Do we in the church need extensive statistical studies? If so, for what purposes? One vital, alive church in California does not even keep a membership role, yet it keeps track of the people who attend. Do churches with membership roles use them to promote fellowship among members?

Chapter 6

1. Relate instances in which plainspokenness has been

effective. Relate instances in which it has not. What makes the difference?

2. "The church is simply filled with the unconverted." Discuss this often-made statement. Could the inadequacies of the church, alluded to in the statement, be attributed in part to a lack of plainspokenness on the part of the clergy and leaders of the church? Explain.

3. If we can be effective with persons by knowing their emotional status, why do we often back off from learning that status?

4. Why must we sometimes enunciate the truth, regardless of the response of people? In what manner are we to enunciate it? (See Ephesians 4:15.)

5. "The tendency of administrators and supervisors to cover up the truth with euphemisms is really nothing other than a case of self-deception—or of ignorance." Discuss.

6. How does the tendency to resort to "white lies" square with the idea that telling the truth is a way of respecting a person's dignity? Discuss.

7. Some older married couples have said, "We have never spoken harsh words or had an argument with each other." Does this statement indicate an ideal relationship? Explain.

Chapter 7

1. Supposing that demon possession is a reality, how could we ever tell that a person was demon-possessed rather than psychotic? Discuss the following statement: "The

whole topic of demon possession is basically not very relevant to us and thus not worth our time. We would be far better off putting our emphasis elsewhere."

2. What sort of treatment and care programs does your community have for the emotionally disturbed and mentally handicapped? What is your church doing to help these people? What additional things could your church do?

3. In what sense do we and can we become "Legion," fragmented persons? How can we become whole?

4. Cite some ways in which the serious pursuit of Christian values could involve you or your church in controversy. For example, could trying to develop adequate programs for the poor, the emotionally crippled, the alcoholic, the released criminal bring your church into conflict with major groups in the community? What if your church established a halfway house for alcoholics or drug users on its property? Perhaps your church has had these conflicts. Discuss them, asking whether the conflicts could have been handled better.

5. Our society is made up of special interest groups with highly paid corps of lobbyists. The groups with the most powerful lobbies seem to be the most influential. Whose interests should the church be most concerned about representing? Does your church need to get more involved in political advocacy? Explain how.

6. What about investments in countries that are oppressive? What are guidelines for deciding whether or not investment is justified? For example, is investment in China acceptable but not investment in South Africa? Explain.

7. Think about your lifestyles. How do you indulge expensive tastes or pursue comfort at another's expense? Is Romans 14:21 relevant to this question? If so, how?

8. How would detachment (from possessions) affect your lifestyle?

9. Has your church been adhering to any secular measures of success? In what ways has your church been pursuing kingdom values? What kingdom values require more attention in your church? How can they be pursued?

Notes

Chapter 1

[1] Adapted from George B. Wall, *Introduction to Ethics* (Columbus, Ohio: Charles E. Merrill Publishing Company, 1974), pp. 1-2. Used by permission.

[2] Blaise Pascal, *Pensées*, trans. W.F. Trotter, Great Books of the Western World, vol. 33 (Chicago: Encyclopaedia Britannica, Inc., 1952), p. 190.

[3] *Ibid.*

[4] Rich Roberts, "Ryun Felt the Pain Again When Decker Fell," *Los Angeles Times* (August 11, 1984), p. 22.

[5] F. Scott Fitzgerald, excerpted from *Three Novels* (New York: Charles Scribner's Sons, 1953), p. 15. Copyright 1953 Charles Scribner's Sons; copyright renewed © 1981 by Malcolm Cowley. Reprinted with permission of Charles Scribner's Sons.

[6] *Ibid.*, p. 90.

Chapter 2

[1] Adin Steinsaltz, *The Essential Talmud*, trans. Chaya Galai (New York: Bantam Books, Inc., 1976), p. 144.

[2] *Ibid.*, p. 139.

[3] George Foot Moore, *Judaism*, Vol. II (Cambridge: Harvard University Press, 1954), p. 129.

[4] *Ibid.*, p. 269.

Chapter 3

[1] Epictetus, *The Enchiridion*, in W. T. Jones, *Approaches to Ethics* (New York: McGraw-Hill Book Company, Inc., 1962), p. 82a.

[2] X. J. Kennedy, ed., *Literature*, 3rd edition (Boston: Little, Brown & Company, 1983), pp. 106-120.

[3] William Styron, *The Confessions of Nat Turner* (New York: Random House, 1966), p. 257.

Chapter 4

[1] Dotson Rader, "And Sometimes He Cries," *Parade* (April 22, 1984), p. 6.

[2] Cervantes, *Don Quixote*, trans. John Ormsby, *The Great Books of the Western World*, vol. 29 (Chicago: Encyclopaedia Britannica, Inc., 1952), p. 261. Reprinted by permission from *The Great Books of the Western World*, copyright 1952 by Encyclopaedia Britannica, Inc.

[3] *Ibid.*, p. 262.

[4] X. J. Kennedy, ed., *Literature*, 3rd edition (Boston: Little, Brown & Company, 1983), pp. 191-229.

[5] Unpublished studies by Newton Maloney, Fuller Theological Seminary, Pasadena, California.

Chapter 5

[1] Timothy Leary, *Flashbacks: An Autobiography* (Boston: Houghton Mifflin Co., J. P. Tarcher, Inc.).

Chapter 6

[1] John may well have had contact with the ascetic community at Qumran, where the Dead Sea Scrolls were found.

Chapter 7

[1] Thomas J. Peters and Robert H. Waterman, Jr., *In Search of Excellence* (New York: Warner Books, 1982), p. 244.

[2] Lynn Horsley, "Failed Farmer Couldn't Face Losing All the Things He Loved," *Houston Chronicle* (May 5, 1985), sec. l, p. 3.

[3] Evan Moore, "Oil Patch Fate Erases Millions," *Houston Chronicle*, (January 27, 1985), sec. 1, pp. 1, 14.